A book of English odes

Frederick Windham Tickner

Nabu Public Domain Reprints:

You are holding a reproduction of an original work published before 1923 that is in the public domain in the United States of America, and possibly other countries. You may freely copy and distribute this work as no entity (individual or corporate) has a copyright on the body of the work. This book may contain prior copyright references, and library stamps (as most of these works were scanned from library copies). These have been scanned and retained as part of the historical artifact.

This book may have occasional imperfections such as missing or blurred pages, poor pictures, errant marks, etc. that were either part of the original artifact, or were introduced by the scanning process. We believe this work is culturally important, and despite the imperfections, have elected to bring it back into print as part of our continuing commitment to the preservation of printed works worldwide. We appreciate your understanding of the imperfections in the preservation process, and hope you enjoy this valuable book.

The KINGS TREASURIES
OF LITERATURE

GENERAL EDITOR
Sir A·T· QUILLER COUCH

JOHN DRYDEN

A BOOK OF ENGLISH ODES

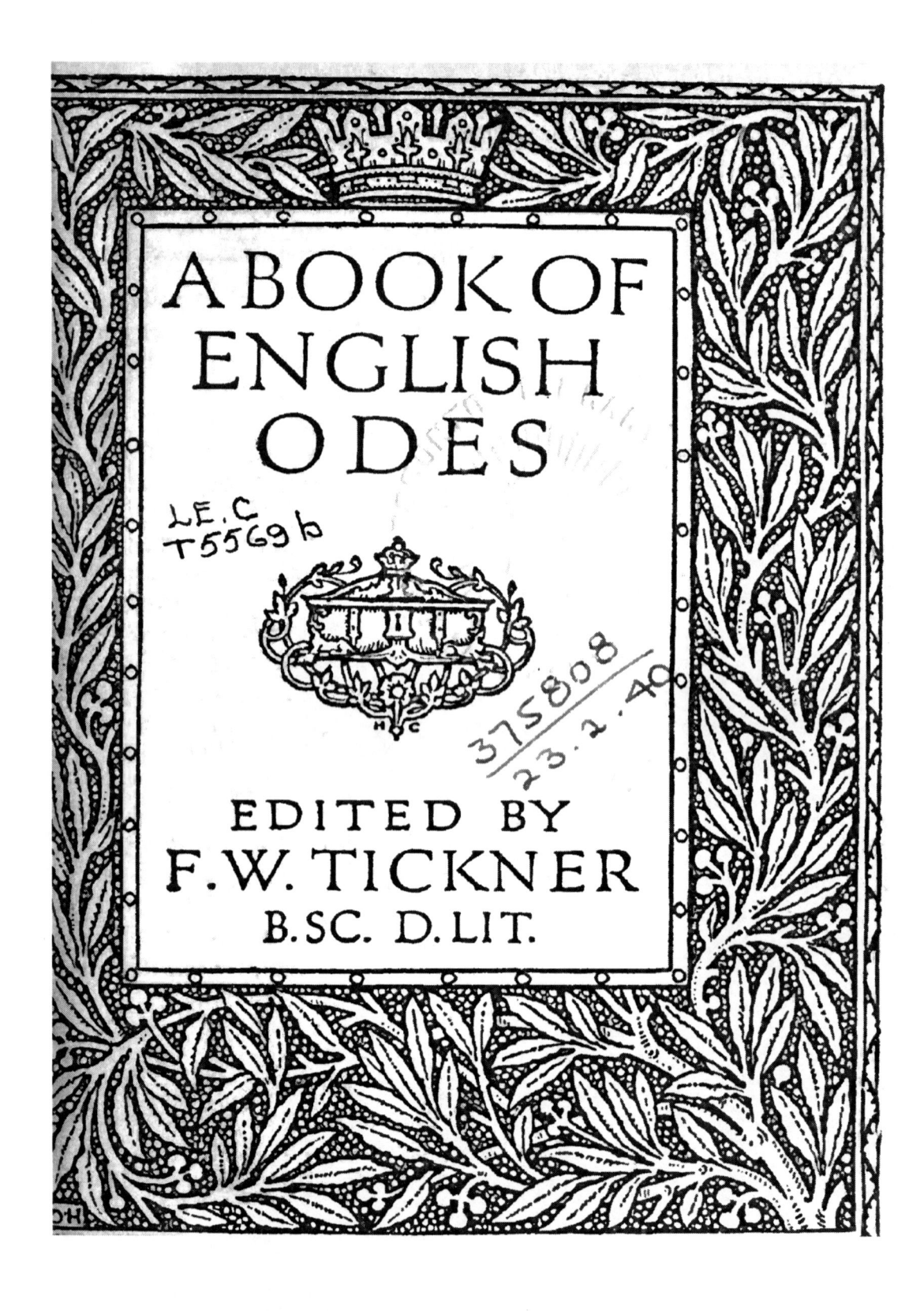

EDITED BY
F. W. TICKNER
B.SC. D.LIT.

All rights reserved

SOLE AGENT FOR SCOTLAND
THE GRANT EDUCATIONAL CO. LTD.
GLASGOW

PRINTED IN GREAT BRITAIN

INTRODUCTION

However diversified in form and in subject-matter the poems in this collection may seem to be, they are all united by the fact that they belong to that particular branch of lyrical poetry to which the name *Ode* is given. As the name suggests, an ode (Greek ᾠδή from ᾄδω to sing) was originally a poem intended to be sung to a musical accompaniment; but the term is now applied to poems which are not written for any such accompaniment, though many modern odes would lend themselves admirably to a musical setting and some of them receive it.

We may well ask then what constitutes an ode in the modern meaning of the term; and the question will perhaps be best answered, for the present at any rate, by describing an ode as a lyrical poem of a stately and elaborate kind, which treats of some important subject in a dignified and exalted style, usually with careful formality of structure and elaborate treatment of versification.

Such a description covers many of the finest poems in our language, poems, too, which are increasing in number as time goes on, for the ode has ever been a favourite medium with modern English poets, in spite of its not always successful use by Poets Laureate.

But students will best realise the almost infinite variety of subject-matter and treatment of which the ode is capable by reading the selections themselves; after they have read these they will be in a better position to inquire into the story of the development of this particular form of verse, and to understand its significance in English poetry.

ACKNOWLEDGMENTS

For permission to use copyright poems, acknowledgments are due, and are gratefully tendered, to:

Mr. ROBERT BRIDGES, THE CLARENDON PRESS, and Messrs. HEINEMANN, for the *Shakespeare Ode*; Mr. T. STURGE MOORE, executor of the author, and Messrs. GEORGE BELL AND SONS, LTD., for Michael Field's *Ode to Dawn*; Mr. JOHN MASEFIELD and Messrs. HEINEMANN for *The Kings go by*; Mr. JOHN LANE and Mr. LASCELLES ABERCROMBIE for *Ceremonial Ode intended for a University*; Rev. F. D. MORICE, for *Translation of a Pindaric Ode*; Messrs. MACMILLAN AND CO., LTD., for Matthew Arnold's *Westminster Abbey*; Messrs. HEINEMANN, LTD., for Swinburne's *Ode on Victor Hugo*; and Messrs. GEORGE BELL AND SONS, LTD., for Coventry Patmore's *Winter*.

CONTENTS

		PAGE
INTRODUCTION		5
PROTHALAMION	*Edmund Spenser*	9
TO HIMSELF	*Ben Jonson*	15
TO MASTER ANTHONY STAFFORD	*Thomas Randolph*	18
ON THE MORNING OF CHRIST'S NATIVITY	*John Milton*	21
BRUTUS	*Abraham Cowley*	30
CROMWELL'S RETURN FROM IRELAND	*Andrew Marvell*	33
TO BEN JONSON	*Robert Herrick*	38
SONG FOR ST. CECILIA'S DAY	*John Dryden*	39
ALEXANDER'S FEAST	*John Dryden*	41
A PINDARIQUE ODE	*William Congreve*	46
TO FEAR	*William Collins*	52
TO EVENING	*William Collins*	55
THE PASSIONS	*William Collins*	57
ON A DISTANT PROSPECT OF ETON COLLEGE	*Thomas Gray*	61
THE PROGRESS OF POESY	*Thomas Gray*	64
THE BARD	*Thomas Gray*	69
ON THE PLEASURE ARISING FROM VICISSITUDE	*Thomas Gray*	74
ODE TO WINTER	*Thomas Campbell*	76
THE BATTLE OF THE BALTIC	*Thomas Campbell*	78
ODE TO DUTY	*William Wordsworth*	81
ON INTIMATIONS OF IMMORTALITY	*William Wordsworth*	83
DEJECTION	*S. T. Coleridge*	90
TO WORDSWORTH	*W. S. Landor*	95

CONTENTS

		PAGE
VENICE	Lord Byron . .	98
TO LIBERTY . . .	P. B. Shelley . .	103
TO THE WEST WIND .	P. B. Shelley . .	113
TO A SKYLARK . .	P. B. Shelley . .	116
ON A GRECIAN URN .	John Keats . .	120
TO A NIGHTINGALE .	John Keats . .	122
TO AUTUMN . . .	John Keats . .	124
ON MELANCHOLY . .	John Keats . .	126
ON THE BEACH AT NIGHT .	Walt Whitman . .	127
ON THE DEATH OF THE DUKE OF WELLINGTON . .	Lord Tennyson . .	129
WESTMINSTER ABBEY . .	Matthew Arnold . .	138
TO THE NORTH-EAST WIND .	Charles Kingsley . .	144
TO VICTOR HUGO . .	A. C. Swinburne . .	147
ODE	A. W. E. O'Shaughnessy .	153
WINTER	Coventry Patmore . .	156
ODE TO DAWN . . .	Michael Field . .	158
THE TERCENTENARY OF SHAKESPEARE . .	Robert Bridges . .	161
THE KINGS GO BY WITH JEWELLED CROWNS .	John Masefield . .	165
ODE INTENDED FOR A UNIVERSITY . . .	Lascelles Abercrombie .	166
COMMENTARY Development of the Ode.		168
QUESTIONS AND EXERCISES		175
APPENDIX Translations of Pindaric and Horatian Odes		187

A BOOK OF ENGLISH ODES

EDMUND SPENSER (1552–1599)

PROTHALAMION

CALM was the day, and through the trembling air
Sweet-breathing Zephyrus did softly play—
A gentle spirit, that lightly did delay
Hot Titan's beams, which then did glister fair;
When I (whom sullen care,
Through discontent of my long fruitless stay
In princes' court, and expectation vain
Of idle hopes, which still do fly away
Like empty shadows, did afflict my brain),
Walk'd forth to ease my pain
Along the shore of silver-streaming Thames;
Whose rutty bank, the which his river hems,
Was painted all with variable flowers,

Prothalamion. This word has no existence in Greek or Latin. The epithalamion was a song composed in honour of a wedding. It besought prosperity to the bride and bridegroom, and was sung after the wedding had taken place. Spenser invented the term "prothalamion" on the analogy of epithalamion to signify a song of greeting to happy lovers before the day of the wedding. This prothalamion was written in honour of the wedding of Elizabeth and Katherine Somerset, the daughters of the Earl of Worcester. Spenser also wrote a beautiful *Epithalamion* to celebrate his own courtship and marriage.

And all the meads adorn'd with dainty gems
Fit to deck maidens' bowers,
And crown their paramours
Against the bridal day, which is not long:
    Sweet Thames! run softly, till I end my song.

There in a meadow by the river's side
A flock of nymphs I chancéd to espy,
All lovely daughters of the flood thereby,
With goodly greenish locks all loose untied
As each had been a bride;
And each one had a little wicker basket
Made of fine twigs, entrailéd curiously,
In which they gather'd flowers to fill their flasket,
And with fine fingers cropt full feateously
The tender stalks on high.
Of every sort which in that meadow grew
They gather'd some; the violet, pallid blue,
The little daisy that at evening closes,
The virgin lily and the primrose true:
With store of vermeil roses,
To deck their bridegrooms' posies
Against the bridal day, which was not long:
    Sweet Thames! run softly, till I end my song.

With that I saw two swans of goodly hue
Come softly swimming down along the lee;
Two fairer birds I yet did never see;
The snow which doth the top of Pindus strow
Did never whiter show,
Nor Jove himself, when he a swan would be
For love of Leda, whiter did appear;
Yet Leda was (they say) as white as he,
Yet not so white as these, nor nothing near;

So purely white they were
That even the gentle stream, the which them bare,
Seem'd foul to them, and bade his billows spare
To wet their silken feathers, lest they might
Soil their fair plumes with water not so fair,
And mar their beauties bright
That shone as Heaven's light
Against heir bridal day, which was not long:
   Sweet Thames! run softly, till I end my song.

Eftsoons the nymphs, which now had flowers their fill,
Ran all in haste to see that silver brood
As they came floating on the crystal flood;
Whom when they saw, they stood amazéd still
Their wondering eyes to fill;
Them seem'd they never saw a sight so fair
Of fowls, so lovely, that they sure did deem
Them heavenly born, or to be that same pair
Which through the sky draw Venus' silver team;
For sure they did not seem
To be begot of any earthly seed,
But rather angels, or of angels' breed;
Yet were they bred of summer's heat, they say,
In sweetest season, when each flower and weed
The earth did fresh array;
So fresh they seem'd as day,
Even as their bridal day, which was not long:
   Sweet Thames! run softly, till I end my song.

Then forth they all out of their baskets drew
Great store of flowers, the honour of the field,
That to the sense did fragrant odours yield,
All which upon those goodly birds they threw
And all the waves did strew,

That like old Peneus' waters they did seem
When down along by pleasant Tempe's shore
Scatter'd with flowers, through Thessaly they stream,
That they appear, through lilies' plenteous store,
Like a bride's chamber-floor.
Two of these nymphs meanwhile two garlands bound
Of freshest flowers which in that mead they found,
The which presenting all in trim array,
Their snowy foreheads therewithal they crown'd;
Whilst one did sing this lay
Prepared against that day,
Against their bridal day, which was not long:
   Sweet Thames! run softly, till I end my song.

"Ye gentle birds! the world's fair ornament,
And Heaven's glory, whom this happy hour
Doth lead unto your lovers' blissful bower,
Joy may you have, and gentle heart's content
Of your love's complement;
And let fair Venus, that is queen of love,
With her heart-quelling son upon you smile,
Whose smile, they say, hath virtue to remove
All love's dislike, and friendship's faulty guile
For ever to assoil.
Let endless peace your steadfast hearts accord,
And blessed plenty wait upon your board;
And let your bed with pleasures chaste abound,
That fruitful issue may to you afford
Which may your foes confound,
And make your joys redound
Upon your bridal day, which is not long:
   Sweet Thames! run softly, till I end my song."

Tempe. A beautiful valley in Thessaly watered by the river Peneus and praised by the poets for its beauty.

So ended she; and all the rest around
To her redoubled that her undersong,
Which said their bridal day should not be long:
And gentle Echo from the neighbour ground
Their accents did resound.
So forth those joyous birds did pass along
Adown the lee that to them murmur'd low,
As he would speak but that he lack'd a tongue,
Yet did by signs his glad affection show,
Making his stream run slow.
And all the fowl which in his flood did dwell
'Gan flock about these twain, that did excel
The rest, so far as Cynthia doth shend
The lesser stars. So they, enrangéd well,
Did on those two attend
And their best service lend
Against their wedding day, which was not long:
   Sweet Thames! run softly, till I end my song.

At length they all to merry London came,
To merry London, my most kindly nurse,
That to me gave this life's first native source,
Though from another place I take my name,
An house of ancient fame:
There when they came whereas those bricky towers
The which on Thames' broad agèd back do ride,
Where now the studious lawyers have their bowers,
There whilome wont the Templar-knights to bide,
Till they decay'd through pride;

   Cynthia. The moon. Cynthus, a mountain of Delos, was the birthplace of Apollo and Diana.
   Bricky towers, etc. The Temple. The *stately place* was the house of the Earl of Essex (situated where Essex Street now stands). It had been inhabited by the great Earl of Leicester, who died in 1588.

Next whereunto there stands a stately place,
Where oft I gainéd gifts and goodly grace
Of that great lord, which therein wont to dwell,
Whose want too well now feels my friendless case;
But ah! here fits not well
Old woes, but joys to tell
Against the bridal day, which is not long:
Sweet Thames! run softly, till I end my song.

Yet therein now doth lodge a noble peer,
Great England's glory and the world's wide wonder,
Whose dreadful name late thro' all Spain did thunder,
And Hercules' two pillars standing near
Did make to quake and fear:
Fair branch of honour, flower of chivalry!
That fillest England with thy triumphs' fame
Joy have thou of thy noble victory,
And endless happiness of thine own name
That promiseth the same;
That through thy prowess and victorious arms
Thy country may be freed from foreign harms,
And great Eliza's glorious name may ring
Through all the world, fill'd with thy wide alarms
Which some brave Muse may sing
To ages following,
Upon the bridal day, which is not long:
  Sweet Thames! run softly, till I end my song.

From those high towers this noble lord issúing
Like radiant Hesper, when his golden hair
In th' ocean billows he hath bathéd fair,

Noble peer. The Earl of Essex, at this time the favourite of Elizabeth, and the leader in 1596 of a successful expedition to Cadiz.

Descended to the river's open viewing
With a great train ensuing.
Above the rest were goodly to be seen
Two gentle knights of lovely face and feature,
Beseeming well the bower of any queen,
With gifts of wit and ornaments of nature,
Fit for so goodly stature,
That like the twins of Jove they seem'd in sight
Which deck the baldric of the Heavens bright;
They two, forth pacing to the river's side,
Received those two fair brides, their love's delight;
Which, at th' appointed tide,
Each one did make his bride
Against their bridal day, which is not long:
  Sweet Thames! run softly, till I end my song.

BEN JONSON (1573–1637)

TO HIMSELF

  Come, leave the loathéd stage,
  And the more loathsome age;
Where pride and impudence, in faction knit,
  Usurp the chair of wit.
Indicting and arraigning every day
  Something they call a play.

Twins. Castor and Pollux; the *baldric* of the heavens is the belt of constellations which forms the Zodiac.

Ben Jonson. After 1625 Jonson, who had written nothing for the stage for nearly ten years, produced some plays which proved failures. It was the lack of success of one of these, *The New Inn*, "never acted, but most negligently played by some, the king's servants, and most squeamishly beheld and censured by others, the king's subjects," that provoked this ode.

    Let their fastidious, vain
    Commission of the brain
Run on and rage, sweat, censure, and condemn;
They were not made for thee, less thou for them.

    Say that thou pour'st them wheat,
    And they will acorns eat;
'Twere simple fury still thyself to waste
    On such as have no taste!
To offer them a surfeit of pure bread
    Whose appetites are dead!
    No, give them grains their fill,
    Husks, draff to drink or swill:
If they love lees, and leave the lusty wine,
Envy them not, their palate's with the swine.

    No doubt some mouldy tale,
    Like Pericles, and stale
As the shrieve's crusts, and nasty as his fish-
    Scraps, out of every dish
Thrown forth, and raked into the common tub,
    May keep up the Play-club;
    There, sweepings do as well
    As the best-ordered meal;
For who the relish of these guests will fit,
Needs set them but the alms-basket of wit.

    And much good do 't you then:
    Brave plush-and-velvet-men
Can feed on orts; and, safe in your stage-clothes,
    Dare quit, upon your oaths,
The stagers and the stage-wrights too, your peers,
    Of larding your large ears

    With their foul comic socks,
    Wrought upon twenty blocks;
Which if they are torn, and turned, and patched enough,
The gamesters share your gilt, and you their stuff.

    Leave things so prostitute,
    And take the Alcaic lute;
Or thine own Horace, or Anacreon's lyre;
    Warm thee by Pindar's fire:
And though thy nerves be shrunk, and blood be cold,
    Ere years have made thee old,
    Strike that disdainful heat
    Throughout, to their defeat,
As curious fools, and envious of thy strain,
May, blushing, swear no palsy's in thy brain.

    But when they hear thee sing
    The glories of thy king,
His zeal to God, and his just awe o'er men;
    They may, blood-shaken then,
Feel such a flesh-quake to possess their powers,
    As they shall cry: "Like ours
    In sound of peace or wars,
    No harp e'er hit the stars,
In tuning forth the acts of his sweet reign,
And raising Charles his chariot 'bove his Wain."

THOMAS RANDOLPH (1605-1635)

TO MASTER ANTHONY STAFFORD TO HASTEN HIM INTO THE COUNTRY

  Come, spur away,
I have no patience for a longer stay,
  But must go down,
And leave the chargeable noise of this great town;
  I will the country see,
  Where old simplicity,
  Though hid in grey,
  Doth look more gay
Than foppery in plush and scarlet clad.
  Farewell, you city wits, that are
  Almost at civil war;
'Tis time that I grow wise, when all the world grows mad.

  More of my days
I will not spend to gain an idiot's praise;
  Or to make sport
For some slight puisne of the Inns-of-Court,
  Then, worthy Stafford, say,
  How shall we spend the day?
  With what delights
  Shorten the nights?
When from this tumult we are got secure,
  Where mirth with all her freedom goes,
  Yet shall no finger lose;
Where every word is thought, and every thought is pure.

 Randolph. This poet was one of the followers of Ben Jonson. He showed much promise as a playwright and poet, but died young with but little accomplished of any great value.
 Puisne. Junior.

      There from the tree
We'll cherries pluck, and pick the strawberry;
      And every day
Go see the wholesome country girls make hay,
      Whose brown hath lovelier grace
      Than any painted face,
      That I do know
      Hyde Park can show,
Where I had rather gain a kiss than meet
  (Though some of them in greater state
    Might court my love with plate)
The beauties of the Cheap, and wives of Lombard Street.

      But think upon
Some other pleasures; these to me are none.
      Why did I prate
Of women, that are things against my fate?
      I never mean to wed
      That torture to my bed.
      My muse is she
      My love shall be.
Let clowns get wealth and heirs; when I am gone,
  And the great bugbear, grisly death,
  Shall take this idle breath,
If I a poem leave, that poem is my son.

      Of this no more;
We'll rather taste the bright Pomona's store.
      No fruit shall 'scape
Our palates, from the damson to the grape,
      Then (full) we'll seek a shade,
      And hear what music's made;
      How Philomel

  Philomel. The nightingale. What is the classical story of Procne and Philomela?

      Her tale doth tell,
And now the other birds do fill the quire;
    The thrush and blackbird lend their throats
    Warbling melodious notes;
We will all sports enjoy which others but desire.

      Ours is the sky,
Whereat what fowl we please our hawk shall fly:
    Nor will we spare
To hunt the crafty fox or timorous hare;
    But let our hounds run loose
    In any ground they'll choose,
    The buck shall fall,
    The stag, and all:
Our pleasures must from their own warrants be,
   For to my muse, if not to me,
   I'm sure all game is free:
Heaven, earth, all are but parts of her great royalty.

     And when we mean
To taste of Bacchus' blessings now and then,
    And drink by stealth
A cup or two to noble Barkley's health,
    I'll take my pipe and try
    The Phrygian melody;
    Which he that hears,
    Lets through his ears
A madness to distemper all the brain.
    Then I another pipe will take
    And Doric music make,
To civilise with graver notes our wits again.

  Phrygian. The Greeks had three chief musical modes or scales, the Doric, grave and majestic; the Phrygian, gay and sprightly; and the Lydian, languishing and tender.

JOHN MILTON (1608–1674)

ODE
ON THE MORNING OF CHRIST'S NATIVITY

This is the month, and this the happy morn,
Wherein the Son of Heaven's Eternal King,
Of wedded maid and virgin mother born,
Our great redemption from above did bring;
For so the holy sages once did sing
That He our deadly forfeit should release,
And with His Father work us a perpetual peace.

That glorious Form, that Light unsufferable,
And that far-beaming blaze of Majesty
Wherewith He wont at Heaven's high council-table
To sit the midst of Trinal Unity,
He laid aside; and, here with us to be,
Forsook the courts of everlasting day,
And chose with us a darksome house of mortal clay.

Say, heavenly Muse, shall not thy sacred vein
Afford a present to the Infant God?
Hast thou no verse, no hymn, or solemn strain
To welcome Him to this His new abode,
Now while the heaven, by the sun's team untrod,
Hath took no print of the approaching light,
And all the spangled host keep watch in squadrons bright?

See how from far, upon the eastern road,
The star-led wizards haste with odours sweet:
O run, prevent them with thy humble ode

Prevent. Get before them; anticipate them.

And lay it lowly at His blessed feet;
Have thou the honour first thy Lord to greet,
And join thy voice unto the angel quire
From out His secret altar touch'd with hallow'd fire.

THE HYMN

It was the winter wild
While the heaven-born Child
All meanly wrapt in the rude manger lies;
Nature in awe to Him
Had doff'd her gaudy trim,
With her great Master so to sympathise:
It was no season then for her
To wanton with the sun, her lusty paramour.

Only with speeches fair
She woos the gentle air
To hide her guilty front with innocent snow;
And on her naked shame,
Pollute with sinful blame,
The saintly veil of maiden white to throw;
Confounded, that her Maker's eyes
Should look so near upon her foul deformities.

But He, her fears to cease,
Sent down the meek-eyed Peace:
She, crown'd with olive green, came softly sliding
Down through the turning sphere,
His ready harbinger,
With turtle wing the amorous clouds dividing;
And waving wide her myrtle wand,
She strikes an universal peace through sea and land.

No war or battle's sound
Was heard the world around:
The idle spear and shield were high unhung;
The hookéd chariot stood
Unstain'd with hostile blood;
The trumpet spake not to the arméd throng;
And kings sat still with awful eye,
As if they surely knew their sovran Lord was by.

But peaceful was the night
Wherein the Prince of Light
His reign of peace upon the earth began:
The winds, with wonder whist,
Smoothly the waters kist,
Whispering new joys to the mild oceán—
Who now hath quite forgot to rave,
While birds of calm sit brooding on the charméd wave.

The stars, with deep amaze,
Stand fix'd in steadfast gaze,
Bending one way their precious influence;
And will not take their flight
For all the morning light,
Or Lucifer that often warn'd them thence;
But in their glimmering orbs did glow
Until their Lord Himself bespake, and bid them go.

And though the shady gloom
Had given day her room,
The sun himself withheld his wonted speed,
And hid his head for shame,
As his inferior flame
The new-enlighten'd world no more should need:
He saw a greater Sun appear
Than his bright throne, or burning axletree, could bear.

The shepherds on the lawn
Or ere the point of dawn
Sate simply chatting in a rustic row;
Full little thought they then
That the mighty Pan
Was kindly come to live with them below;
Perhaps their loves, or else their sheep,
Was all that did their silly thoughts so busy keep.

When such music sweet
Their hearts and ears did greet
As never was by mortal finger strook—
Divinely-warbled voice
Answering the stringéd noise,
As all their souls in blissful rapture took:
The air, such pleasure loth to lose,
With thousand echoes still prolongs each heavenly close.

Nature that heard such sound
Beneath the hollow round
Of Cynthia's seat the airy region thrilling,
Now was almost won
To think her part was done,
And that her reign had here its last fulfilling;
She knew such harmony alone
Could hold all heaven and earth in happier union.

At last surrounds their sight
A globe of circular light
That with long beams the shamefaced night array'd;
The helméd Cherubim
And sworded Seraphim
Are seen in glittering ranks with wings display'd,
Harping in loud and solemn quire
With unexpressive notes, to Heaven's new-born Heir.

ENGLISH ODES

Such music (as 'tis said)
Before was never made
But when of old the sons of morning sung,
While the Creator great
His constellations set
And the well-balanced world on hinges hung;
And cast the dark foundations deep,
And bid the weltering waves their oozy channel keep.

Ring out, ye crystal spheres!
Once bless our human ears,
If ye have power to touch our senses so;
And let your silver chime
Move in melodious time;
And let the base of heaven's deep organ blow;
And with your ninefold harmony
Make up full consort to the angelic symphony.

For if such holy song
Enwrap our fancy long,
Time will run back, and fetch the age of gold;
And speckled vanity
Will sicken soon and die,
And leprous sin will melt from earthly mould;
And Hell itself will pass away,
And leave her dolorous mansions to the peering day.

Yea, Truth and Justice then
Will down return to men,
Orb'd in a rainbow; and, like glories wearing,
Mercy will sit between,
Throned in celestial sheen,
With radiant feet the tissued clouds down steering;
And Heaven, as at some festival,
Will open wide the gates of her high palace hall.

But wisest Fate says No;
This must not yet be so;
The Babe yet lies in smiling infancy
That on the bitter cross
Must redeem our loss;
So both Himself and us to glorify:
Yet first, to those ychain'd in sleep
The wakeful trump of doom must thunder through the deep:

With such a horrid clang
As on Mount Sinai rang
While the red fire and smouldering clouds outbrake:
The aged Earth aghast
With terror of that blast
Shall from the surface to the centre shake,
When, at the world's last session,
The dreadful Judge in middle air shall spread His throne.

And then at last our bliss
Full and perfect is,
But now begins; for from this happy day
The old Dragon under ground,
In straiter limits bound,
Not half so far casts his usurpéd sway;
And, wroth to see his kingdom fail,
Swinges the scaly horror of his folded tail.

The oracles are dumb;
No voice or hideous hum
Runs through the archéd roof in words deceiving:
Apollo from his shrine
Can no more divine,
With hollow shriek the steep of Delphos leaving:

No nightly trance or breathéd spell
Inspires the pale-eyed priest from the prophetic cell.

The lonely mountains o'er
And the resounding shore
A voice of weeping heard, and loud lament;
From haunted spring and dale
Edged with poplar pale
The parting Genius is with sighing sent;
With flower-inwoven tresses torn
The nymphs in twilight shade of tangled thickets mourn.

In consecrated earth
And on the holy hearth
The Lars and Lemures moan with midnight plaint;
In urns, and altars round,
A drear and dying sound
Affrights the Flamens at their service quaint;
And the chill marble seems to sweat,
While each peculiar Power forgoes his wonted seat.

Peor and Baalim
Forsake their temples dim,
With that twice-batter'd god of Palestine;
And moonéd Ashtaroth
Heaven's queen and mother both,
Now sits not girt with tapers' holy shine;
The Libyc Hammon shrinks his horn,
In vain the Tyrian maids their wounded Thammuz mourn.

And sullen Moloch, fled,
Hath left in shadows dread
His burning idol all of blackest hue;

In vain with cymbals' ring
They call the grisly king,
In dismal dance about the furnace blue;
The brutish gods of Nile as fast,
Isis, and Orus, and the dog Anubis, haste.

Nor is Osiris seen
In Memphian grove, or green,
Trampling the unshower'd grass with lowings loud;
Nor can he be at rest
Within his sacred chest;
Nought but profoundest hell can be his shroud;
In vain with timbrell'd anthems dark
The sable-stoléd sorcerers bear his worshipt ark.

He feels from Juda's land
The dreaded Infant's hand;
The rays of Bethlehem blind his dusky eyn;
Nor all the gods beside
Longer dare abide,
Nor Typhon huge ending in snaky twine:
Our Babe, to show His Godhead true,
Can in His swaddling bands control the damnéd crew.

So, when the sun in bed
Curtain'd with cloudy red
Pillows his chin upon an orient wave,
The flocking shadows pale
Troop to the infernal jail,
Each fetter'd ghost slips to his several grave;
And the yellow-skirted fays
Fly after the night-steeds, leaving their moon-loved maze.

But see, the Virgin blest
Hath laid her Babe to rest;
Time is our tedious song should here have ending:
Heaven's youngest-teeméd star
Hath fix'd her polish'd car,
Her sleeping Lord with hand-maid lamp attending:
And all about the courtly stable
Bright-harness'd angels sit in order serviceable.

AT A SOLEMN MUSIC

BLEST pair of Sirens, pledges of Heaven's joy,
Sphere-born harmonious Sisters, Voice and Verse!
Wed your divine sounds, and mixt power employ,
Dead things with inbreathed sense able to pierce;
And to our high-raised phantasy present
That undisturbéd Song of pure concent
Aye sung before the sapphire-colour'd throne
    To Him that sits thereon.
With saintly shout and solemn jubilee;
Where the bright Seraphim in burning row
Their loud uplifted angel-trumpets blow;
And the Cherubic host in thousand quires
Touch their immortal harps of golden wires,
With those just Spirits that wear victorious palms,
    Hymns devout and holy psalms
    Singing everlastingly:
That we on earth, with undiscording voice
May rightly answer that melodious noise;
As once we did, till disproportion'd sin
Jarr'd against nature's chime, and with harsh din

Concent. Not consent, but *concentus*, harmony.

Broke the fair music that all creatures made
To their great Lord, whose love their motion sway'd
In perfect diapason, whilst they stood
In first obedience, and their state of good.
O may we soon again renew that Song,
And keep in tune with Heaven, till God ere long
To His celestial concert us unite,
To live with Him, and sing in endless morn of light!

ABRAHAM COWLEY (1618–1667)

BRUTUS

EXCELLENT Brutus, of all human race
The best till nature was improved by grace,
Till men above themselves faith raiséd more
    Than reason above beasts before;
Virtue was thy life's centre, and from thence
Did silently and constantly dispense
    The gentle vigorous influence
To all the wide and fair circumference;
And all the parts upon it lean'd so easily,
Obey'd the mighty force so willingly,
That none could discord or disorder see
    In all their contrariety;
Each had his motion natural and free,
And the whole no more moved than the whole world
    could be.

From thy strict rule some think that thou didst swerve
(Mistaken honest men) in Cæsar's blood;
What mercy could thy tyrants' life deserve,
From him who kill'd himself rather than serve?

ENGLISH ODES

    Th' heroic exaltations of good
    Are so far from understood,
We count them vice: alas, our sight's so ill,
That things which swiftest move seem to stand still.
We look not upon virtue in her height,
On her supreme idea, brave and bright,
    In the original light:
    But as her beams reflected pass
Through our own nature or ill custom's glass.
    And 'tis no wonder so,
    If with dejected eye
  In standing pools we seek the sky,
That stars so high above should seem to us below.

    Can we stand by and see
Our mother robb'd and bound, and ravish'd be,
    Yet not to her assistance stir,
Pleas'd with the strength and beauty of the ravisher?
Or shall we fear to kill him, if before
    The cancell'd name of friend he bore?
    Ungrateful Brutus do they call?
Ungrateful Cæsar who could Rome enthrall!
An act more barbarous and unnatural
(In th' exact balance of true virtue tried)
Than his successor Nero's parricide!
    There's none but Brutus could deserve
    That all men else should wish to serve,
And Cæsar's usurped place to him should proffer;
None can deserve 't but he who would refuse the offer.

Ill fate assumed a body thee t'affright,
And wrapped itself i' th' terrors of the night,
I'll meet thee at Philippi, said the sprite;

> I'll meet thee there, saidst thou,
> With such a voice, and such a brow,
As put the trembling ghost to sudden flight.
> It vanished as a taper's light
> Goes out when spirits appear in sight.
One would have thought 't had heard the morning crow,
Or seen her well-appointed star
Come marching up the eastern hill afar.
Nor durst it in Philippi's field appear,
> But unseen attacked thee there.
Had it presumed in any shape thee to oppose,
Thou wouldst have forced it back upon thy foes:
> Or slain 't like Cæsar, though it be
A conqueror and a monarch mightier far than he.

What joy can human things to us afford,
When we see perish thus by odd events,
> Ill men, and wretched accidents,
The best cause and best man that ever drew a sword?
> When we see
The false Octavius, and wild Antony,
> Godlike Brutus, conquer thee?
What can we say but thine own tragic word,
That virtue, which had worshipped been by thee
As the most solid good, and greatest deity,
> By this fatal proof became
> An idol only, and a name?
Hold, noble Brutus, and restrain
The bold voice of thy generous disdain:
> These mighty gulfs are yet
Too deep for all thy judgment and thy wit.
The time's set forth already which shall quell
Stiff reason, when it offers to rebel;

Which these great secrets shall unseal,
And new philosophies reveal.
A few years more, so soon hadst thou not died,
Would have confounded human virtue's pride,
And shew'd thee a God crucified.

ANDREW MARVELL (1621–1678)

HORATIAN ODE UPON CROMWELL'S RETURN FROM IRELAND

THE forward youth that would appear,
Must now forsake his Muses dear,
    Nor in the shadows sing
    His numbers languishing.

'Tis time to leave the books in dust,
And oil the unuséd armour's rust,
    Removing from the wall
    The corslet of the hall.

So restless Cromwell could not cease
In the inglorious arts of peace,
    But through adventurous war
    Urgéd his active star:

And like the three-fork'd lightning first,
Breaking the clouds where it was nurst,
    Did thorough his own side
    His fiery way divide:

Horatian Ode. "Better than anything else in our language this poem gives an idea of a grand Horatian measure, as well as of the diction and spirit of an Horatian ode."—GOLDWIN SMITH.

For 'tis all one to courage high
The emulous, or enemy;
　　And with such, to enclose
　　Is more than to oppose.

Then burning through the air he went
And palaces and temples rent;
　　And Cæsar's head at last
　　Did through his laurels blast.

'Tis madness to resist or blame
The face of angry heaven's flame;
　　And if we would speak true,
　　Much to the Man is due

Who, from his private gardens, where
He lived reservéd and austere
　　(As if his highest plot
　　To plant the bergamot),

Could by industrious valour climb
To ruin the great work of time,
　　And cast the Kingdoms old
　　Into another mould.

Though Justice against Fate complain,
And plead the ancient Rights in vain—
　　But those do hold or break
　　As men are strong or weak.

For 'tis all one, etc. Expand this so as to make the meaning clearer.

Nature, that hateth emptiness,
Allows of penetration less,
    And therefore must make room
    Where greater spirits come.

What field of all the civil war
Where his were not the deepest scar?
    And Hampton shows what part
    He had of wiser art,

Where, twining subtle fears with hope,
He wove a net of such a scope
    That Charles himself might chase
    To Carisbrook's narrow case;

That thence the Royal actor borne
The tragic scaffold might adorn:
    While round the arméd bands
    Did clap their bloody hands;

He nothing common did or mean
Upon that memorable scene,
    But with his keener eye
    The axe's edge did try;

Nor call'd the Gods, with vulgar spite,
To vindicate his helpless right;
    But bow'd his comely head
    Down, as upon a bed.

  Nature, etc. I.e. Nature abhors a vacuum; matter must occupy space.
  Hampton. Hampton Court where Charles was a prisoner of the Parliament.

—This was that memorable hour
Which first assured the forcéd power:
    So when they did design
    The Capitol's first line,

A Bleeding Head, where they begun,
Did fright the architects to run;
    And yet in that the State
    Foresaw its happy fate!

And now the Irish are ashamed
To see themselves in one year tamed:
    So much one man can do
    That does both act and know.

They can affirm his praises best,
And have, though overcome, confest
    How good he is, how just
    And fit for highest trust;

Nor yet grown stiffer with command,
But still in the Republic's hand—
    How fit he is to sway
    That can so well obey!

He to the Commons' feet presents
A Kingdom for his first year's rents,
    And (what he may) forbears
    His fame, to make it theirs:

And has his sword and spoils ungirt
To lay them at the Public's skirt.
    So when the falcon high
    Fails heavy from the sky,

She, having kill'd, no more does search
But on the next green bough to perch,
    Where, when he first does lure,
    The falconer has her sure.

—What may not then our Isle presume
While victory his crest does plume?
    What may not others fear
    It thus he crowns each year!

As Cæsar he, ere long, to Gaul,
To Italy an Hannibal,
    And to all states not free
    Shall climacteric be.

The Pict no shelter now shall find
Within his parti-colour'd mind,
    But from this valour sad,
    Shrink underneath the plaid—

Happy, if in the tufted brake
The English hunter him mistake,
    Nor lay his hounds in near
    The Caledonian deer.

But Thou, the War's and Fortune's son,
March indefatigably on;
    And for the last effect
    Still keep the sword erect:

Besides the force it has to fright
The spirits of the shady night,
    The same arts that did gain
    A power, must it maintain.

ROBERT HERRICK (1591–1674)

TO BEN JONSON

Ah Ben,
Say how, or when
Shall we thy Guests
Meet at those Lyric Feasts,
Made at the Sun,
The Dog, the Triple Tun?
Where we such clusters had,
As made us nobly wild, not mad;
And yet each Verse of thine
Outdid the meat, outdid the frolic wine.

My Ben,
Or come again,
Or send to us,
Thy wit's great over-plus;
But teach us yet
Wisely to husband it;
Lest we that talent spend:
And having once brought to an end
That precious stock; the store
Of such a wit the world should have no more.

JOHN DRYDEN (1631-1700)

SONG FOR ST. CECILIA'S DAY

From Harmony, from heavenly Harmony
    This universal frame began:
When Nature underneath a heap
    Of jarring atoms lay
And could not heave her head,
The tuneful voice was heard from high:
    Arise, ye more than dead!
Then cold, and hot, and moist, and dry
    In order to their stations leap,
    And Music's power obey.
From harmony, from heavenly harmony
    This universal frame began:
    From harmony to harmony
Through all the compass of the notes it ran,
The diapason closing full in Man.

What passion cannot Music raise and quell?
    When Jubal struck the chorded shell
    His listening brethren stood around,
    And, wondering, on their faces fell
    To worship that celestial sound.
Less than a god they thought there could not dwell

Song for St. Cecilia's Day. Both this and the following ode were written for the festival of St. Cecilia; this one for the year 1687, the second for the year 1697. The story of St. Cecilia is well known.

Cold and hot, etc. The allusion is to the four "elements" of the Greeks—earth, air, fire and water.

Within the hollow of that shell
That spoke so sweetly and so well.
What passion cannot Music raise and quell?

The trumpet's loud clangour
  Excites us to arms,
With shrill notes of anger
  And mortal alarms.
The double double double beat
  Of the thundering drum
Cries "Hark! the foes come;
Charge, charge, 'tis too late to retreat!"

The soft complaining flute
In dying notes discovers
The woes of hopeless lovers,
Whose dirge is whisper'd by the warbling lute.

Sharp violins proclaim
Their jealous pangs and desperation,
Fury, frantic indignation,
Depth of pains, and height of passion
  For the fair disdainful dame.

But oh! what art can teach,
What human voice can reach
  The sacred organ's praise?
Notes inspiring holy love,
Notes that wing their heavenly ways
  To mend the choirs above.

Orpheus could lead the savage race,
And trees uprooted left their place

Sequacious of the lyre:
But bright Cecilia raised the wonder higher:
When to her Organ vocal breath was given
An Angel heard, and straight appear'd—
   Mistaking Earth for Heaven!

Grand Chorus

As from the power of sacred lays
   The spheres began to move,
And sung the great Creator's praise
   To all the blest above;

So when the last and dreadful hour
This crumbling pageant shall devour,
The trumpet shall be heard on high,
The dead shall live, the living die,
And Music shall untune the sky.

ALEXANDER'S FEAST
OR, THE POWER OF MUSIC

'Twas at the royal feast for Persia won
   By Philip's warlike son—
Aloft in awful state
The godlike hero sate
On his imperial throne;
His valiant peers were placed around,
Their brows with roses and with myrtles bound
(So should desert in arms be crown'd);
The lovely Thais by his side
Sate like a blooming eastern bride
In flower of youth and beauty's pride:—

Happy, happy, happy pair!
None but the brave,
None but the brave,
None but the brave deserves the fair!

Timotheus placed on high
Amid the tuneful quire
With flying fingers touch'd the lyre:
The trembling notes ascend the sky
And heavenly joys inspire.
The song began from Jove
Who left his blissful seats above—
Such is the power of mighty love!
A dragon's fiery form belied the god;
Sublime on radiant spires he rode
When he to fair Olympia prest,
And while he sought her snowy breast,
Then round her slender waist he curl'd,
And stamp'd an image of himself, a sovereign of the world.
—The listening crowd admire the lofty sound!
A present deity! they shout around:
A present deity! the vaulted roofs rebound!
With ravish'd ears
The monarch hears,
Assumes the god;
Affects to nod
And seems to shake the spheres.

The praise of Bacchus then the sweet musician sung,
Of Bacchus ever fair and ever young;

Timotheus was really a great flute-player of the court of Alexander the Great.

ENGLISH ODES

The jolly god in triumph comes!
Sound the trumpets, beat the drums!
Flush'd with a purple grace
He shows his honest face:
Now give the hautboys breath; he comes, he comes!
Bacchus, ever fair and young,
Drinking joys did first ordain;
Bacchus' blessings are a treasure,
Drinking is the soldier's pleasure;
Rich the treasure,
Sweet the pleasure,
Sweet is pleasure after pain.

    Soothed with the sound, the king grew vain;
Fought all his battles o'er again,
And thrice he routed all his foes, and thrice he slew the slain!
The master saw the madness rise,
His glowing cheeks, his ardent eyes;
And while he Heaven and Earth defied
Changed his hand and check'd his pride.
He chose a mournful Muse
Soft pity to infuse:
He sung Darius great and good,
By too severe a fate
Fallen, fallen, fallen, fallen,
Fallen from his high estate,
And weltering in his blood;
Deserted, at his utmost need,
By those his former bounty fed;
On the bare earth exposed he lies
With not a friend to close his eyes.
—With downcast looks the joyless victor sate,
Revolving in his alter'd soul

The various turns of Chance below;
And now and then a sigh he stole,
And tears began to flow.

   The mighty master smiled to see
That love was in the next degree;
'Twas but a kindred-sound to move,
For pity melts the mind to love.
Softly sweet, in Lydian measures
Soon he soothed his soul to pleasures.
War, he sung, is toil and trouble,
Honour but an empty bubble;
Never ending, still beginning,
Fighting still, and still destroying;
If the world be worth thy winning,
Think, O think, it worth enjoying;
Lovely Thais sits beside thee,
Take the good the gods provide thee!
—The many rend the skies with loud applause:
So Love was crown'd, but Music won the cause.
The prince, unable to conceal his pain,
Gazed on the fair
Who caused his care,
And sigh'd and look'd, sigh'd and look'd,
Sigh'd and look'd, and sigh'd again:
At length with love and wine at once opprest
The vanquish'd victor sunk upon her breast.

   Now strike the golden lyre again:
A louder yet, and yet a louder strain!
Break his bands of sleep asunder
And rouse him like a rattling peal of thunder.
Hark, hark! the horrid sound
Has raised up his head:

ENGLISH ODES

As awaked from the dead
And amazed he stares around.
Revenge, revenge, Timotheus cries,
See the Furies arise!
See the snakes that they rear
How they hiss in their hair,
And the sparkles that flash from their eyes!
Behold a ghastly band,
Each a torch in his hand!
Those are Grecian ghosts, that in battle were slain
And unburied remain
Inglorious on the plain:
Give the vengeance due
To the valiant crew!
Behold how they toss their torches on high
How they point to the Persian abodes
And glittering temples of their hostile gods.
—The princes applaud with a furious joy:
And the King seized a flambeau with zeal to destroy;
Thais led the way
To light him to his prey,
And like another Helen, fired another Troy!

—Thus, long ago,
Ere heaving bellows learn'd to blow,
While organs yet were mute,
Timotheus, to his breathing flute
And sounding lyre
Could swell the soul to rage, or kindle soft desire.
At last divine Cecilia came,
Inventress of the vocal frame;
The sweet enthusiast from her sacred store
Enlarged the former narrow bounds,
And added length to solemn sounds,

With Nature's mother-wit, and arts unknown before.
—Let old Timotheus yield the prize
Or both divide the crown;
He raised a mortal to the skies;
She drew an angel down!

WILLIAM CONGREVE (1670–1729)

A PINDARIQUE ODE

HUMBLY OFFERED TO THE QUEEN, ON THE VICTORIOUS PROGRESS OF HER MAJESTY'S ARMS UNDER THE CONDUCT OF THE DUKE OF MARLBOROUGH.

I

DAUGHTER of Memory, Immortal Muse
Calliope; what poet wilt thou chuse
   Of ANNA's name to sing?
  To whom wilt thou thy Fire impart,
   Thy Lyre, thy Voice, and tuneful Art;
Whom raise sublime on thy Aetherial Wing,
And consecrate with Dews of thy Castalian Spring?

II

Without thy Aid, the most aspiring Mind
Must flag beneath, to narrow Flights confin'd,

A Pindarique Ode. Congreve was the first English poet to understand the true character of the Pindaric ode. Unfortunately his practice was not equal to his theory; but this ode is of interest as the first English ode to be constructed on the true Pindaric model. The student will return to this ode after reading the Commentary at the end of the book.

ENGLISH ODES

      Striving to rise in vain:
  Nor e'er can hope with equal Lays
  To celebrate bright Virtue's Praise.
Thy Aid obtain'd, even I, the humblest Swain,
May climb Pierian Heights, and quit the lowly Plain.

III

High in the Starry Orb is hung,
And next *Alcides* Guardian Arm,
That Harp to which thy *Orpheus* Sung,
  Who Woods, and Rocks, and Winds cou'd Charm,
That Harp which on *Cyllene's* shady Hill,
  When first the vocal Shell was found,
      With more than Mortal Skill
  Inventer *Hermes* taught to found.
Hermes on bright *Latona's* Son,
    By sweet Persuasion won,
    The wondrous Work bestow'd;
    Latona's Son, to thine
  Indulgent, gave the Gift Divine:
A God the Gift, a God th' Invention show'd.

I

To that high-sounding Lyre I tune my Strains;
A lower Note his lofty Song disdains
    Who sings of ANNA's Name.
  The Lyre is struck, the Sounds I hear.
  O Muse, propitious to my Pray'r.
O well-known Sounds. O Melody, the same
That kindled *Mantuan* Fire and raised *Mæonian* Flame.

II

Nor are these Sounds to *British* Bards unknown,
Or sparingly reveal'd to one alone:
   Witness sweet *Spencer's* Lays:
  And witness that Immortal Song,
   As *Spencer* sweet, as *Milton* strong,
Which humble Boyn o'er Tiber's Flood cou'd raise,
And mighty *William* Sing, with well-proportion'd Praise.

III

  Rise, Fair *Augusta*, lift thy Head,
  With Golden Tow'rs thy Front adorn;
  Come forth, as comes from *Tithon's* Bed
  With cheerful Ray the ruddy Morn.
Thy lovely Form, and fresh reviving State,
  In Crystal Flood of *Thames* survey;
    Then, bless thy better Fate,
  Bless ANNA's most Auspicious Sway.
  While distant Realms and neighb'ring Lands,
    Arm'd Troops and hostile Bands
    On ev'ry Side molest,
    Thy happier Clime is Free
  Fair CAPITAL of Liberty.
And Plenty knows, and Days of Halcyon Rest.

I

As *Britain's* Isle, when old vex'd Ocean roars,
Unshaken sees against her Silver Shores
    His foaming Billows beat;
  So *Britain's* QUEEN, amidst the Jars
  And Tumults of a World in Wars,
Fix'd on the Base of Her well-founded State,
Serene and safe Looks down, nor feels the Shocks of Fate.

II

But Greatest Souls, tho' blest with sweet Repose,
Are soonest touch'd with Sense of other Woes.
    Thus ANNA's mighty Mind,
    To Mercy and soft Pity prone,
    And mov'd with Sorrows not her own,
Has all her Peace and downy Rest resign'd,
To wake for Common Good, and succour Humankind.

III

Fly, Tyranny, no more be known
Within *Europa's* blissful Bound;
Far as th' unhabitable Zone
Fly ev'ry hospitable Ground.
To horrid *Zembla's* Frozen Realms repair,
    There with the baleful Beldam, NIGHT,
        Unpeopl'd Empire share,
    And rob *those* Lands of Legal Right.
For now is come the promis'd Hour,
    When Justice shall have Pow'r;
Justice to Earth restor'd!
    Again *Astrea* Reigns!
ANNA Her equal Scale maintains,
And MARLBRO wields Her sure deciding Sword.

I

Now, coud'st thou soar, my Muse, to Sing the MAN
In heights sublime, as when the *Mantuan* Swan
    Her tow'ring Pinions spread;
    Thou should'st of MARLBRO Sing, whose Hand
    Unerring from his QUEEN's Command,
Far as the Seven-mouth'd *Ister's* secret Head,
To save th' Imperial State, Her hardy *Britons* led.

II

Nor there thy Song should end; tho' all the Nine
Might well their Harps and Heav'nly Voices join
  To Sing that Glorious Day,
 When Bold *Bavaria* fled the Field,
 And Veteran *Gauls* unus'd to yield,
 On *Blenheim's* Plain imploring Mercy lay;
And Spoils and Trophies won, perplex'd the Victor's way.

III

 But cou'd thy Voice of *Blenheim* Sing,
 And with Success that Song pursue;
 What Art cou'd Aid thy weary Wing
 To keep the Victor still in view?
For as the Sun ne'er stops his radiant Flight,
 Nor Sets, but with impartial Ray
  To all who want his Light
 Alternately transfers the Day:
So in the Glorious Round of Fame,
 . Great MARLBRO, still the same,
  Incessant runs his Course;
 His Conqu'ring Arms by turns appear,
And Universal is his Aid and Force.

I

Attempt not to proceed, unwary Muse,
For O, what Notes, what Numbers cou'dst thou chuse,
  Tho' in all Numbers skill'd;
 To Sing the Hero's matchless Deed,
 Which *Belgia* Sav'd, and *Brabant* Free'd;
To Sing *Ramillia's* Day, to which must yield
Cannæ's Illustrious Fight, and Fam'd Pharsalia's Field.

ENGLISH ODES

II

In the short Course of a Diurnal Sun,
Behold the Work of many Ages done!
    What verse such Worth can Raise?
  Lustre and Life, the Poet's Art
  To middle Virtue may impart;
But Deeds sublime, exalted high like These,
Transcend his utmost Flight; and mock his distant Praise.

III

  Still wou'd the willing Muse aspire
  With transport still her Strains prolong;
  But Fear unstrings the trembling Lyre,
  And Admiration stops her Song.
Go on, Great Chief, in ANNA's Cause proceed;
  Nor sheath the Terrors of thy Sword
    Till *Europe* thou hast freed,
  And Universal Peace restor'd.
  This mighty Work when thou shalt End,
    Equal Rewards attend,
    Of Value far above
    Thy Trophies and Thy Spoils;
  Rewards even Worthy of thy Toils,
Thy QUEEN's just Favour, and thy COUNTRY's Love.

WILLIAM COLLINS (1721–1759)

TO FEAR

Thou, to whom the world unknown,
With all its shadowy shapes, is shown;
Who seest, appalled, the unreal scene,
While fancy lifts the veil between:
    Ah Fear! ah frantic Fear!
    I see, I see thee near.
I know thy hurried step, thy haggard eye!
Like thee I start; like thee disordered fly.
For, lo, what monsters in thy train appear!
Danger, whose limbs of giant mould
What mortal eye can fixed behold?
Who stalks his round, an hideous form,
Howling amidst the midnight storm;
Or throws him on the ridgy steep
Of some loose hanging rock to sleep:
And with him thousand phantoms joined,
Who prompt to deeds accursed the mind:
And those, the fiends, who, near allied,
O'er Nature's wounds, and wrecks, preside;
Whilst vengeance, in the lurid air,
Lifts her red arm, exposed and bare;
On whom that ravening brood of Fate,
Who lap the blood of sorrow, wait:
Who, Fear, this ghastly train can see,
And look not madly wild, like thee?

ENGLISH ODES

EPODE

In earliest Greece, to thee, with partial choice,
    The grief-full muse addrest her infant tongue;
The maids and matrons, on her awful voice,
    Silent and pale, in wild amazement hung.

Yet he, the bard who first invoked thy name,
    Disdained in Marathon its power to feel:
For not alone he nursed the poet's flame,
    But reached from Virtue's hand the patriot's steel.

But who is he whom later garlands grace,
    Who left awhile o'er Hybla's dews to rove,
With trembling eyes thy dreary steps to trace,
    Where thou and furies shared the baleful grove?

Wrapt in thy cloudy veil, the incestuous queen
    Sighed the sad call her son and husband heard,
When once alone it broke the silent scene,
    And he, the wretch of Thebes, no more appeared.

O Fear, I know thee by my throbbing heart:
    Thy withering power inspired each mournful line:
Though gentle Pity claim her mingled part,
    Yet all the thunders of the scene are thine!

The bard. Æschylus, who fought in the battle of Marathon.
He whom later garlands grace. Sophocles.
The incestuous queen is Jocasta, mother and wife of Oedipus. The story of their terrible fate is told by Sophocles in his *Oedipus Tyrannus*.

ANTISTROPHE

Thou who such weary lengths hast past,
Where wilt thou rest, mad Nymph, at last?
Say, wilt thou shroud in haunted cell,
Where gloomy rape and murder dwell?
    Or, in some hollowed seat,
    'Gainst which the big waves beat,
Hear drowning seamen's cries, in tempests brought?
Dark power, with shuddering meek submitted thought,
Be mine to read the visions old
Which thy awakening bards have told:
And, lest thou meet my blasted view,
Hold each strange tale devoutly true;
Ne'er be I found, by thee o'erawed,
In that thrice hallowed eve, abroad,
When ghosts, as cottage maids believe,
Their pebbled beds permitted leave;
And goblins haunt, from fire, or fen,
Or mine, or flood, the walks of men!

    O thou, whose spirit most possest
The sacred seat of Shakespeare's breast!
By all that from thy prophet broke,
In thy divine emotions spoke;
Hither again thy fury deal,
Teach me but once like him to feel;
His cypress wreath my meed decree,
And I, O Fear, will dwell with thee!

TO EVENING

If aught of oaten stop or pastoral song
May hope, chaste Eve, to soothe thy modest ear
    Like thy own solemn springs,
    Thy springs, and dying gales:

O Nymph reserved,—while now the bright-hair'd sun
Sits in yon western tent, whose cloudy skirts,
    With brede ethereal wove,
    O'erhang his wavy bed,

Now air is hush'd, save where the weak-eyed bat
With short shrill shriek flits by on leathern wing,
    Or where the beetle winds
    His small but sullen horn,

As oft he rises 'midst the twilight path,
Against the pilgrim borne in heedless hum,—
    Now teach me, maid composed,
    To breathe some soften'd strain

Whose numbers, stealing through my dark'ning vale,
May not unseemly with its stillness suit:
    As musing slow I hail
    Thy genial loved return.

For when thy folding-star arising shows
His paly circlet, at his warning lamp
    The fragrant Hours, and Elves
    Who slept in buds the day,

And many a Nymph who wreathes her brows with sedge
And sheds the freshening dew, and lovelier still
    The pensive Pleasures sweet,
    Prepare thy shadowy car.

Then let me rove some wild and heathy scene;
Or find some ruin midst its dreary dells,
    Whose walls more awful nod
    By thy religious gleams.

Or if chill blustering winds or driving rain
Prevent my willing feet, be mine the hut
    That, from the mountain's side,
    Views wilds and swelling floods,

And hamlets brown, and dim-discover'd spires;
And hears their simple bell; and marks o'er all
    Thy dewy fingers draw
    The gradual dusky veil.

While Spring shall pour his showers, as oft he wont,
And bathe thy breathing tresses, meekest Eve!
    While Summer loves to sport
    Beneath thy lingering light;

While sallow Autumn fills thy lap with leaves;
Or Winter, yelling through the troublous air,
    Affrights thy shrinking train
    And rudely rends thy robes;

So long, regardful of thy quiet rule,
Shall Fancy, Friendship, Science, smiling Peace,
    Thy gentlest influence own,
    And love thy favourite name!

THE PASSIONS
An Ode for Music

When Music, heavenly maid, was young,
While yet in early Greece she sung,
The Passions oft, to hear her shell,
Throng'd around her magic cell
Exulting, trembling, raging, fainting,
Possest beyond the Muse's painting;
By turns they felt the glowing mind
Disturb'd, delighted, raised, refined:
'Till once, 'tis said, when all were fired,
Fill'd with fury, rapt, inspired,
From the supporting myrtles round
They snatch'd her instruments of sound,
And, as they oft had heard apart
Sweet lessons of her forceful art,
Each (for madness ruled the hour)
Would prove his own expressive power.

First Fear his hand, its skill to try,
   Amid the chords bewilder'd laid,
And back recoil'd, he knew not why,
   E'en at the sound himself had made.

Next Anger rushed, his eyes on fire,
   In lightnings owned his secret stings;
In one rude clash he struck the lyre
   And swept with hurried hand the strings.

With woeful measures wan Despair—
   Low sullen sounds his grief beguiled,
A solemn, strange, and mingled air,
   'Twas sad by fits, by starts 'twas wild.

But thou, O Hope, with eyes so fair,
   What was thy delighted measure?
Still it whisper'd promised pleasure
   And bade the lovely scenes at distance hail!

Still would her touch the strain prolong;
   And from the rocks, the woods, the vale
She call'd on Echo still through all the song;
   And, where her sweetest theme she chose,
   A soft responsive voice was heard at every close;
And Hope enchanted smiled, and waved her golden hair:—

And longer had she sung:—but with a frown
    Revenge impatient rose:
He threw his blood-stain'd sword in thunder down;
    And with a withering look
   The war-denouncing trumpet took,
And blew a blast so loud and dread,
Were ne'er prophetic sounds so full of woe!
    And ever and anon he beat
    The doubling drum with furious heat;
And, though sometimes, each dreary pause between,
    Dejected Pity at his side,
    Her soul-subduing voice applied,
   Yet still he kept his wild unaltered mien,
While each strained ball of sight seem'd bursting from
    his head.

Thy numbers, Jealousy, to nought were fixed:
   Sad proof of thy distressful state!
Of differing themes the veering song was mixed;
   And now it courted Love, now raving called on Hate.

With eyes up-raised, as one inspired,
Pale Melancholy sat retired;
And from her wild sequestered seat,
In notes by distance made more sweet,
Pour'd through the mellow horn her pensive soul:
    And dashing soft from rocks around
    Bubbling runnels joined the sound;
Through glades and glooms the mingled measure stole,
  Or, o'er some haunted stream, with fond delay,
    Round an holy calm diffusing,
    Love of peace, and lonely musing,
In hollow murmurs died away.

But O! how alter'd was its sprightlier tone
When Cheerfulness, a nymph of healthiest hue,
  Her bow across her shoulder flung,
  Her buskins gemm'd with morning dew,
Blew an inspiring air, that dale and thicket rung,
  The hunter's call to Faun and Dryad known!
The oak-crown'd Sisters and their chaste-eyed Queen,
  Satyrs and Sylvan Boys, were seen
  Peeping from forth their alleys green:
Brown Exercise rejoiced to hear;
  And Sport leapt up, and seized his beechen spear.

Last came Joy's ecstatic trial:
He, with viny crown advancing,
  First to the lively pipe his hand addrest:
But soon he saw the brisk awakening viol
  Whose sweet entrancing voice he loved the best:
They would have thought who heard the strain
    They saw, in Tempe's vale, her native maids
    Amidst the festal-sounding shades

To some unwearied minstrel dancing
　　While, as his flying fingers kiss'd the strings,
　　　Love framed with Mirth a gay fantastic round:
　　　Loose were her tresses seen, her zone unbound;
　　　And he, amidst his frolic play,
　　　As if he would the charming air repay,
　　Shook thousand odours from his dewy wings.

　　　O Music! sphere-descended maid,
　　　Friend of Pleasure, Wisdom's aid!
　　　Why, goddess, why, to us denied,
　　　Lay'st thou thy ancient lyre aside?
　　　As in that loved Athenian bower
　　　You learn'd an all-commanding power,
　　　Thy mimic soul, O nymph endear'd,
　　　Can well recall what then it heard.
　　　Where is thy native simple heart
　　　Devote to Virtue, Fancy, Art?
　　　Arise, as in that elder time,
　　　Warm, energetic, chaste, sublime!
　　　Thy wonders, in that god-like age,
　　　Fill thy recording Sister's page—
　　　'Tis said, and I believe the tale,
　　　Thy humblest reed could more prevail,
　　　Had more of strength, diviner rage,
　　　Than all which charms this laggard age;
　　　E'en all at once together found
　　　Cecilia's mingled world of sound—
　　　O bid our vain endeavours cease:
　　　Revive the just designs of Greece:
　　　Return in all thy simple state!
　　　Confirm the tales her sons relate!

THOMAS GRAY (1716–1771)

ODE
ON A DISTANT PROSPECT OF ETON COLLEGE

Ye distant spires, ye antique towers
   That crown the watery glade,
Where grateful Science still adores
   Her Henry's holy shade;
And ye, that from the stately brow
Of Windsor's heights th' expanse below
Of grove, of lawn, of mead survey,
Whose turf, whose shade, whose flowers among
Wanders the hoary Thames along
   His silver-winding way:

Ah happy hills! ah pleasing shade!
   Ah fields beloved in vain!
Where once my careless childhood stray'd,
   A stranger yet to pain!
I feel the gales that from ye blow
A momentary bliss bestow,
As waving fresh their gladsome wing
My weary soul they seem to soothe,
And redolent of joy and youth,
   To breathe a second spring.

Say, Father Thames, for thou hast seen
   Full many a sprightly race
Disporting on thy margent green
   The paths of pleasure trace;

Who foremost now delight to cleave
With pliant arm, thy glassy wave?
The captive linnet which enthrall?
What idle progeny succeed
To chase the rolling circle's speed
   Or urge the flying ball?

While some on earnest business bent
   Their murmuring labours ply
'Gainst graver hours, that bring constraint
   To sweeten liberty:
Some bold adventurers disdain
The limits of their little reign,
And unknown regions dare descry;
Still as they run they look behind,
They hear a voice in every wind,
   And snatch a fearful joy.

Gay hope is theirs by fancy fed,
   Less pleasing when possest;
The tear forgot as soon as shed,
   The sunshine of the breast:
Theirs buxom health, of rosy hue,
Wild wit, invention ever new,
And lively cheer, of vigour born;
The thoughtless day, the easy night,
The spirits pure, the slumbers light
   That fly th' approach of morn.

Alas! regardless of their doom
   The little victims play!
No sense have they of ills to come
   Nor care beyond to-day:

Yet see how all around 'em wait
The ministers of human fate,
And black Misfortune's baleful train!
Ah show them where in ambush stand
To seize their prey, the murtherous band!
  Ah, tell them they are men!

These shall the fury Passions tear,
  The vultures of the mind,
Disdainful Anger, pallid Fear,
  And Shame that skulks behind:
Or pining Love shall waste their youth,
Or Jealousy with rankling tooth
That inly gnaws the secret heart,
And Envy wan, and faded Care,
Grim-visaged comfortless Despair,
  And Sorrow's piercing dart.

Ambition this shall tempt to rise,
  Then whirl the wretch from high
To bitter Scorn a sacrifice
  And grinning Infamy.
The stings of Falsehood those shall try,
And hard Unkindness' alter'd eye,
That mocks the tear it forced to flow;
And keen Remorse with blood defiled,
And moody Madness laughing wild
  Amid severest woe.

Lo, in the vale of years beneath
  A grisly troop are seen,
The painful family of Death,
  More hideous than their queen:

This racks the joints, this fires the veins.
That every labouring sinew strains,
Those in the deeper vitals rage;
Lo, Poverty, to fill the band,
That numbs the soul with icy hand,
   And slow-consuming Age.

To each his sufferings: all are men,
   Condemn'd alike to groan;
The tender for another's pain,
   The unfeeling for his own.
Yet, ah! why should they know their fate?
Since sorrow never comes too late,
And happiness too swiftly flies.
Thought would destroy their paradise!
No more;—where ignorance is bliss,
   'Tis folly to be wise.

THE PROGRESS OF POESY

A Pindaric Ode

I. 1

Awake, Æolian lyre, awake,
And give to rapture all thy trembling strings.
From Helicon's harmonious springs
   A thousand rills their mazy progress take;
The laughing flowers that round them blow
Drink life and fragrance as they flow.
Now the rich stream of music winds along
Deep, majestic, smooth, and strong,

ENGLISH ODES

Through verdant vales, and Ceres' golden reign;
Now rolling down the steep amain
Headlong, impetuous, see it pour:
The rocks and nodding groves re-bellow to the roar.

I. 2

O Sovereign of the willing soul,
Parent of sweet and solemn-breathing airs,
Enchanting shell! the sullen Cares
   And frantic Passions hear thy soft control.
On Thracia's hills the Lord of War
Has curb'd the fury of his car
And dropt his thirsty lance at thy command.
Perching on the sceptred hand
Of Jove, thy magic lulls the feather'd king
With ruffled plumes, and flagging wing:
Quench'd in dark clouds of slumber lie
The terror of his beak, and lightnings of his eye.

I. 3

Thee the voice, the dance, obey
Temper'd to thy warbled lay.
O'er Idalia's velvet-green
The rosy-crownéd Loves are seen
On Cytherea's day,
With antic Sport, and blue-eyed Pleasures,
Frisking light in frolic measures;

I. 2. Gray wrote that this stanza was intended to express the power of harmony to calm the turbulent sallies of the soul. The thoughts are borrowed from Pindar.

I. 3. To suggest the power of harmony to produce all the graces of motion in the body.

Now pursuing, now retreating,
   Now in circling troops they meet:
To brisk notes in cadence beating
   Glance their many-twinkling feet.
Slow melting strains their Queen's approach declare:
   Where'er she turns the Graces homage pay:
With arms sublime that float upon the air
   In gliding state she wins her easy way:
O'er her warm cheek and rising bosom move
The bloom of young Desire and purple light of Love.

II. 1

   Man's feeble race what ills await!
Labour, and Penury, the racks of Pain,
Disease, and Sorrow's weeping train,
   And Death, sad refuge from the storms of Fate!
The fond complaint, my Song, disprove,
And justify the laws of Jove.
Say, has he given in vain the heavenly Muse?
Night, and all her sickly dews,
Her spectres wan, and birds of boding cry
He gives to range the dreary sky:
Till down the eastern cliffs afar
Hyperion's march they spy, and glittering shafts of war.

II. 2

   In climes beyond the solar road
Where shaggy forms o'er ice-built mountains roam,
The Muse has broke the twilight gloom
   To cheer the shivering native's dull abode.
And oft, beneath the odorous shade
Of Chili's boundless forests laid,

ENGLISH ODES

She deigns to hear the savage youth repeat,
In loose numbers wildly sweet,
Their feather-cinctured chiefs, and dusky loves.
Her track, where'er the Goddess roves,
Glory pursue, and generous Shame,
Th' unconquerable Mind, and Freedom's holy flame.

II. 3

Woods that wave o'er Delphi's steep,
Isles that crown th' Ægean deep,
Fields that cool Ilissus laves,
Or where Mæander's amber waves
In lingering labyrinths creep,
How do your tuneful echoes languish,
Mute, but to the voice of Anguish!
Where each old poetic mountain
   Inspiration breathed around;
Every shade and hallow'd fountain
   Murmur'd deep a solemn sound:
Till the sad Nine, in Greece's evil hour,
   Left their Parnassus for the Latian plains.
Alike they scorn the pomp of tyrant Power,
   And coward Vice, that revels in her chains.
When Latium had her lofty spirit lost,
They sought, O Albion! next, thy sea-encircled coast.

III. 1

  Far from the sun and summer-gale
In thy green lap was Nature's Darling laid,
What time, where lucid Avon stray'd,
  To him the mighty mother did unveil
Her awful face: the dauntless Child
Stretch'd forth his little arms, and smiled.

This pencil take (she said) whose colours clear
Richly paint the vernal year:
Thine, too, these golden keys, immortal Boy!
This can unlock the gates of Joy;
Of Horror that, and thrilling Fears,
Or ope the sacred source of sympathetic Tears.

III. 2

Nor second He, that rode sublime
Upon the seraph-wings of Ecstasy
The secrets of the Abyss to spy:
   He pass'd the flaming bounds of Place and Time:
The living Throne, the sapphire-blaze
Where Angels tremble while they gaze,
He saw; but blasted with excess of light,
Closed his eyes in endless night.
Behold where Dryden's less presumptuous car
Wide o'er the fields of Glory bear
Two Coursers of ethereal race
With necks in thunder clothed, and long-resounding pace.

III. 3

Hark, his hands the lyre explore!
Bright-eyed Fancy, hovering o'er,
Scatters from her pictured urn
Thoughts that breathe, and words that burn.
But ah! 'tis heard no more——
O! Lyre divine, what daring Spirit
Wakes thee now! Tho' he inherit
Nor the pride, nor ample pinion,
   That the Theban Eagle bear,

Two coursers, etc. Dryden's heroic couplet.

Sailing with supreme dominion
  Thro' the azure deep of air:
Yet oft before his infant eyes would run
  Such forms as glitter in the Muse's ray
With orient hues, unborrow'd of the Sun:
  Yet shall he mount, and keep his distant way
Beyond the limits of a vulgar fate:
Beneath the Good how far—but far above the Great.

THE BARD

A Pindaric Ode

I. 1

"RUIN seize thee, ruthless King!
  Confusion on thy banners wait!
Tho' fann'd by Conquest's crimson wing,
  They mock the air with idle state.
Helm, nor hauberk's twisted mail,
Nor e'en thy virtues, tyrant, shall avail
To save thy secret soul from nightly fears,
From Cambria's curse, from Cambria's tears!"
—Such were the sounds that o'er the crested pride
  Of the first Edward scatter'd wild dismay,
As down the steep of Snowdon's shaggy side
  He wound with toilsome march his long array.
Stout Glo'ster stood aghast in speechless trance;
"To arms!" cried Mortimer, and couch'd his quivering
    lance.

The Bard. This ode is founded on a tradition that Edward I., when conquering the Welsh, ordered all the bards to be put to death.

I. 2

On a rock, whose haughty brow
Frowns o'er old Conway's foaming flood,
   Robed in the sable garb of woe,
With haggard eyes the Poet stood;
(Loose his beard and hoary hair
Stream'd like a meteor to the troubled air)
And with a master's hand and prophet's fire
Struck the deep sorrows of his lyre.
  "Hark, how each giant oak and desert-cave
   Sighs to the torrent's awful voice beneath!
O'er thee, O King! their hundred arms they wave,
   Revenge on thee in hoarser murmurs breathe;
Vocal no more, since Cambria's fatal day,
To high-born Hoel's harp, or soft Llewellyn's lay.

I. 3

"Cold is Cadwallo's tongue,
   That hush'd the stormy main:
Brave Urien sleeps upon his craggy bed:
   Mountains, ye mourn in vain
   Modred, whose magic song
Made huge Plinlimmon bow his cloud-topt head.
   On dreary Arvon's shore they lie
Smear'd with gore and ghastly pale;
Far, far aloof the affrighted ravens sail;
   The famish'd eagle screams, and passes by.
Dear lost companions of my tuneful art,
   Dear as the light that visits these sad eyes,
Dear as the ruddy drops that warm my heart,
   Ye died amidst your dying country's cries—

Hoel, *etc.*, are names of famous Welsh bards.

No more I weep. They do not sleep;
   On yonder cliffs, a grisly band,
I see them sit; they linger yet,
   Avengers of their native land:
With me in dreadful harmony they join,
And weave with bloody hands the tissue of thy line.

II. 1

"Weave the warp and weave the woof,
   The winding-sheet of Edward's race:
Give ample room and verge enough
   The characters of hell to trace.
Mark the year and mark the night
When Severn shall re-echo with affright
The shrieks of death thro' Berkley's roof that ring,
Shrieks of an agonising king!
   She-Wolf of France, with unrelenting fangs
That tear'st the bowels of thy mangled mate,
   From thee be born, who o'er thy country hangs
The scourge of Heaven! What Terrors round him wait!
Amazement in his van, with Flight combined,
And Sorrow's faded form, and Solitude behind.

II. 2

"Mighty victor, mighty lord,
Low on his funeral couch he lies!
   No pitying heart, no eye, afford
A tear to grace his obsequies.
Is the sable warrior fled?
Thy son is gone. He rests among the Dead.
The Swarm that in thy noon-tide beam were born?
—Gone to salute the rising Morn.
Fair laughs the Morn, and soft the zephyr blows,

While proudly riding o'er the azure realm
In gallant trim the gilded Vessel goes:
  Youth on the prow, and Pleasure at the helm:
Regardless of the sweeping Whirlwind's sway,
That hush'd in grim repose expects his evening prey.

II. 3

"Fill high the sparkling bowl,
The rich repast prepare;
  Reft of a crown, he yet may share the feast:
Close by the regal chair
  Fell Thirst and Famine scowl
  A baleful smile upon their baffled Guest.
Heard ye the din of battle bray,
  Lance to lance, and horse to horse?
  Long years of havoc urge their destined course,
And thro' the kindred squadrons mow their way.
  Ye Towers of Julius, London's lasting shame,
With many a foul and midnight murther fed,
  Revere his Consort's faith, his Father's fame,
And spare the meek Usurper's holy head!
Above, below, the rose of snow,
  Twined with her blushing foe, we spread:
The bristled Boar in infant-gore
  Wallows beneath the thorny shade.
Now, brothers, bending o'er the accursèd loom,
Stamp we our vengeance deep, and ratify his doom.

III. 1

"Edward, lo! to sudden fate
  (Weave we the woof. The thread is spun.)
Half of thy heart we consecrate.
  (The web is wove. The work is done).

Stay, O stay! nor thus forlorn
Leave me unbless'd, unpitied, here to mourn:
In yon bright track that fires the western skies
They melt, they vanish from my eyes.
But O! what solemn scenes on Snowdon's height
    Descending slow their glittering skirts unroll?
Visions of glory, spare my aching sight,
    Ye unborn Ages, crowd not on my soul!
No more our long-lost Arthur we bewail;—
All hail, ye genuine Kings! Britannia's Issue, hail!

III. 2

"Girt with many a Baron bold
Sublime their starry fronts they rear;
    And gorgeous Dames and Statesmen old
In bearded majesty, appear.
In the midst a Form divine!
Her eye proclaims her of the Briton-Line:
Her lion-port, her awe-commanding face
Attemper'd sweet to virgin grace.
What strings symphonious tremble in the air,
    What strains of vocal transport round her play.
Hear from the grave, great Taliessin, hear;
    They breathe a soul to animate thy clay.
Bright Rapture calls, and soaring as she sings,
Waves in the eye of Heaven her many-colour'd wings.

III. 3

"The verse adorn again
    Fierce War, and faithful Love,
And Truth severe, by fairy Fiction drest.
    In buskin'd measures move

Buskin'd measures. The reference is to Shakespeare; the voice refers to Milton and his *Paradise Lost*; the distant warblings are those of the poets who succeeded him.

Pale Grief, and pleasing Pain,
With Horror, Tyrant of the throbbing breast.
A Voice as of the Cherub-Choir
  Gales from blooming Eden bear,
  And distant warblings lessen on my ear,
That lost in long futurity expire.
Fond impious man, think'st thou yon sanguine cloud,
  Raised by thy breath, has quench'd the Orb of day?
To-morrow he repairs the golden flood,
  And warms the nations with redoubled ray.
Enough for me: with joy I see
  The different doom our Fates assign:
Be thine Despair and sceptred Care;
  To triumph and to die are mine."
—He spoke, and headlong from the mountain's height
Deep in the roaring tide he plunged to endless night.

ODE ON THE PLEASURE ARISING FROM VICISSITUDE

A FRAGMENT

Now the golden Morn aloft
  Waves her dew-bespangled wing,
With vermeil cheek and whisper soft
  She woos the tardy Spring:
Till April starts, and calls around
The sleeping fragrance from the ground,
And lightly o'er the living scene
Scatters his freshest, tenderest green.

Ode on the Pleasure, etc. This ode was left unfinished.

New-born flocks in rustic dance,
  Frisking ply their feeble feet;
Forgetful of their wintry trance
  The birds his presence greet:
But chief, the sky-lark warbles high
His trembling thrilling ecstasy;
And lessening from the dazzled sight,
Melts into air and liquid light.

Yesterday the sullen year
  Saw the snowy whirlwind fly;
Mute was the music of the air,
  The Herd stood drooping by:
Their raptures now that wildly flow
No yesterday nor morrow know;
'Tis man alone that joy descries
With forward and reverted eyes.

Smiles on past Misfortune's brow
  Soft Reflection's hand can trace,
And o'er the cheek of Sorrow throw
  A melancholy grace;
While Hope prolongs our happier hour,
Or deepest shades, that dimly lour
And blacken round our weary way,
Gilds with a gleam of distant day.

Still, where rosy Pleasure leads,
  See a kindred Grief pursue;
Behind the steps that Misery treads
  Approaching Comfort view:
The hues of bliss more brightly glow
Chastised by sabler tints of woe.
And blended form, with artful strife,
The strength and harmony of Life.

See the Wretch that long has tost
   On the thorny bed of Pain,
At length repair his vigour lost
   And breathe and walk again:
The meanest floweret of the vale,
The simplest note that swells the gale,
The common sun, the air, the skies,
To him are opening Paradise.

THOMAS CAMPBELL (1777-1844)

ODE TO WINTER

WHEN first the fiery-mantled Sun
His heavenly race began to run,
Round the earth and ocean blue
His children four the Seasons flew:—
   First, in green apparel dancing,
The young Spring smiled with angel-grace;
   Rosy Summer, next advancing,
Rush'd into her sire's embrace—
Her bright-hair'd sire, who bade her keep
   For ever nearest to his smiles,
On Calpe's olive-shaded steep
   Or India's citron-cover'd isles.
More remote, and buxom-brown,
   The Queen of vintage bow'd before his throne;
A rich pomegranate gemm'd her crown,
   A ripe sheaf bound her zone.

Calpe. Gibraltar.

But howling Winter fled afar
To hills that prop the polar star;
And loves on deer-borne car to ride
With barren darkness at his side,
Round the shore where loud Lofoden
  Whirls to death the roaring whale,
Round the hall where Runic Odin
Howls his war-song to the gale—
Save when adown the ravaged globe
  He travels on his native storm,
Deflowering Nature's grassy robe
  And trampling on her faded form;
Till light's returning Lord assume
  The shaft that drives him to his northern field,
Of power to pierce his raven plume
  And crystal-cover'd shield.

O sire of storms! whose savage ear
The Lapland drum delights to hear,
When Frenzy with her bloodshot eye
Implores thy dreadful deity—
Archangel! Power of desolation!
  Fast descending as thou art,
Say, hath mortal invocation
  Spells to touch thy stony heart:
Then, sullen Winter! hear my prayer,
And gently rule the ruin'd year;
Nor chill the wanderer's bosom bare
Nor freeze the wretch's falling tear:
To shuddering Want's unmantled bed
  Thy horror-breathing agues cease to lend,
And gently on the orphan head
  Of Innocence descend.

But chiefly spare, O king of clouds!
The sailor on his airy shrouds,
When wrecks and beacons strew the steep
And spectres walk along the deep.
   Milder yet thy snowy breezes
   Pour on yonder tented shores,
Where the Rhine's broad billow freezes,
   Or the dark brown Danube roars.
O winds of Winter! list ye there
   To many a deep and dying groan?
Or start, ye demons of the midnight air,
   At shrieks and thunders louder than your own?
Alas! e'en your unhallow'd breath
   May spare the victim fallen low;
But Man will ask no truce to death,
   No bounds to human woe.

THE BATTLE OF THE BALTIC

Of Nelson and the North
Sing the glorious day's renown,
When to battle fierce came forth
All the might of Denmark's crown,
And her arms along the deep proudly shone;
By each gun the lighted brand
In a bold determined hand,
And the Prince of all the land
Led them on.

Like leviathans afloat
Lay their bulwarks on the brine;
While the sign of battle flew
On the lofty British line:

It was ten of April morn by the chime;
As they drifted on their path
There was silence deep as death;
And the boldest held his breath
For a time.

But the might of England flush'd
To anticipate the scene;
And her van the fleeter rush'd
O'er the deadly space between.
"Hearts of oak!" our captains cried, when each gun
From its adamantine lips
Spread a death-shade round the ships,
Like the hurricane eclipse
Of the sun.

Again! again! again!
And the havoc did not slack,
Till a feeble cheer the Dane
To our cheering sent us back;—
Their shots along the deep slowly boom:—
Then ceased—and all is wail,
As they strike the shatter'd sail;
Or in conflagration pale
Light the gloom.

Out spoke the victor then,
As he hail'd them o'er the wave:
"Ye are brothers! ye are men!
And we conquer but to save:—
So peace instead of death let us bring:
But yield, proud foe, thy fleet
With the crews, at England's feet,
And make submission meet
To our King."

Then Denmark blest our chief
That he gave her wounds repose;
And the sounds of joy and grief
From her people wildly rose,
As death withdrew his shades from the day:
While the sun look'd smiling bright
O'er a wide and woeful sight,
Where the fires of funeral light
Died away.

Now joy, old England, raise,
For the tidings of thy might,
By the festal cities' blaze,
Whilst the wine-cup shines in light;
And yet amidst that joy and uproar,
Let us think of them that sleep
Full many a fathom deep
By thy wild and stormy steep,
Elsinore!

Brave hearts! to Britain's pride
Once so faithful and so true,
On the deck of fame that died
With the gallant good Riou:
Soft sigh the winds of heaven o'er their grave!
While the billow mournful rolls
And the mermaid's song condoles
Singing glory to the souls
Of the brave.

WILLIAM WORDSWORTH (1770–1850)

ODE TO DUTY

Stern Daughter of the Voice of God!
O Duty! if that name thou love
Who art a light to guide, a rod
To check the erring, and reprove;
Thou who art victory and law
When empty terrors overawe;
From vain temptations dost set free,
And calm'st the weary strife of frail humanity!

There are who ask not if thine eye
Be on them; who, in love and truth
Where no misgiving is, rely
Upon the genial sense of youth:
Glad hearts! without reproach or blot,
Who do thy work, and know it not:
O! if through confidence misplaced
They fail, thy saving arms, dread Power! around them cast.

Serene will be our days and bright,
And happy will our nature be,
When love is an unerring light,
And joy its own security.
And they a blissful course may hold
Ev'n now who, not unwisely bold,
Live in the spirit of this creed;
Yet seek thy firm support, according to their need.

I, loving freedom, and untried,
No sport of every random gust,
Yet being to myself a guide,
Too blindly have reposed my trust:
And oft, when in my heart was heard
Thy timely mandate, I deferr'd
The task, in smoother walks to stray;
But thee I now would serve more strictly, if I may.

Through no disturbance of my soul
Or strong compunction in me wrought,
I supplicate for thy control,
But in the quietness of thought;
Me this uncharter'd freedom tires;
I feel the weight of chance desires:
My hopes no more must change their name;
I long for a repose that ever is the same.

Stern Lawgiver! yet thou dost wear
The Godhead's most benignant grace;
Nor know we anything so fair
As is the smile upon thy face:
Flowers laugh before thee on their beds,
And fragrance in thy footing treads;
Thou dost preserve the Stars from wrong;
And the most ancient Heavens, through Thee, are fresh and strong.

To humbler functions, awful Power!
I call thee: I myself commend
Unto thy guidance from this hour;
O let my weakness have an end!

Give unto me, made lowly wise,
The spirit of self-sacrifice;
The confidence of reason give;
And in the light of truth thy Bondman let me live.

ODE ON INTIMATIONS OF IMMORTALITY FROM RECOLLECTIONS OF EARLY CHILDHOOD

There was a time when meadow, grove, and stream,
The earth, and every common sight
  To me did seem
  Apparell'd in celestial light,
The glory and the freshness of a dream.
It is not now as it hath been of yore;—
  Turn wheresoe'er I may,
   By night or day,
The things which I have seen I now can see no more.

  The rainbow comes and goes,
  And lovely is the rose;
  The moon doth with delight
Look round her when the heavens are bare;
  Waters on a starry night
  Are beautiful and fair;
The sunshine is a glorious birth;
But yet I know, where'er I go,
That there hath past away a glory from the earth.

Now, while the birds thus sing a joyous song,
    And while the young lambs bound
       As to the tabor's sound,
To me alone there came a thought of grief:
A timely utterance gave that thought relief,
    And I again am strong.
The cataracts blow their trumpets from the steep,—
No more shall grief of mine the season wrong:
I hear the echoes through the mountains throng,
The winds come to me from the fields of sleep,
    And all the earth is gay;
      Land and sea
Give themselves up to jollity,
    And with the heart of May
Doth every beast keep holiday;—
     Thou child of joy
Shout round me, let me hear thy shouts, thou happy
   Shepherd-boy!

Ye blessèd Creatures, I have heard the call
    Ye to each other make; I see
The heavens laugh with you in your jubilee;
    My heart is at your festival,
     My head hath its coronal,
The fullness of your bliss, I feel—I feel it all.
     O evil day! if I were sullen
      While Earth herself is adorning
       This sweet May-morning;
     And the children are culling
       On every side
     In a thousand valleys far and wide
     Fresh flowers; while the sun shines warm,
And the babe leaps up on his mother's arm:—
    I hear, I hear, with joy I hear!
    —But there's a tree, of many, one,

A single field which I have look'd upon,
Both of them speak of something that is gone:
      The pansy at my feet
      Doth the same tale repeat:
Whither is fled the visionary gleam?
Where is it now, the glory and the dream?

Our birth is but a sleep and a forgetting;
The Soul that rises with us, our life's Star,
      Hath had elsewhere its setting
        And cometh from afar;
      Not in entire forgetfulness,
      And not in utter nakedness,
But trailing clouds of glory do we come
      From God, who is our home:
Heaven lies about us in our infancy!
Shades of the prison-house begin to close
      Upon the growing Boy,
But he beholds the light, and whence it flows,
      He sees it in his joy;
The Youth, who daily farther from the east
    Must travel, still is Nature's priest,
      And by the vision splendid
      Is on his way attended;
At length the Man perceives it die away,
And fade into the light of common day.

Earth fills her lap with pleasures of her own;
Yearnings she hath in her own natural kind,
And, even with something of a mother's mind
      And no unworthy aim,
      The homely nurse doth all she can
To make her foster-child, her inmate, Man,
      Forget the glories he hath known,
And that imperial palace whence he came.

Behold the Child among his new-born blisses,
A six-years' darling of a pigmy size!
See, where 'mid work of his own hand he lies,
Fretted by sallies of his mother's kisses,
With light upon him from his father's eyes!
See, at his feet, some little plan or chart,
Some fragment from his dream of human life,
Shaped by himself with newly-learnéd art;
    A wedding or a festival,
    A mourning or a funeral;
    And this hath now his heart,
    And unto this he frames his song;
    Then will he fit his tongue
To dialogues of business, love, or strife;
    But it will not be long
    Ere this be thrown aside,
    And with new joy and pride
The little actor cons another part;
Filling from time to time his "humorous stage"
With all the Persons, down to palsied Age,
That Life brings with her in her equipage;
    As if his whole vocation
    Were endless imitation.

Thou, whose exterior semblance doth belie
    Thy soul's immensity;
Thou best philosopher, who yet dost keep
Thy heritage, thou eye among the blind,
That deaf and silent, read'st the eternal deep,
Haunted for ever by the eternal Mind,—
    Mighty Prophet! Seer blest!
    On whom those truths do rest
Which we are toiling all our lives to find,

In darkness lost, the darkness of the grave;
Thou, over whom thy Immortality
Broods like the day, a master o'er a slave,
A Presence which is not to be put by;
Thou little child, yet glorious in the might
Of heaven-born freedom on thy being's height,
Why with such earnest pains dost thou provoke
The years to bring the inevitable yoke,
Thus blindly with thy blessedness at strife?
Full soon thy soul shall have her earthly freight,
And custom lie upon thee with a weight
Heavy as frost, and deep almost as life!

      O joy! that in our embers
      Is something that doth live,
      That Nature yet remembers
      What was so fugitive!
The thought of our past years in me doth breed
Perpetual benediction: not indeed
  For that which is most worthy to be blest,
Delight and liberty, the simple creed
Of Childhood, whether busy or at rest,
With new-fledged hope still fluttering in his breast:—
      —Not for these I raise
      The song of thanks and praise;
    But for those obstinate questionings
    Of sense and outward things,
    Fallings from us, vanishings,
    Blank misgivings of a creature
Moving about in worlds not realised,
High instincts, before which our mortal nature
Did tremble like a guilty thing surprised:
    But for those first affec ions,
    Those shadowy recollections,

Which, be they what they may,
Are yet the fountain-light of all our day,
Are yet a master-light of all our seeing;
    Uphold us—cherish—and have power to make
Our noisy years seem moments in the being
Of the eternal Silence; truths that wake,
        To perish never;
Which neither listlessness, nor mad endeavour,
      Nor man nor boy,
Nor all that is at enmity with joy,
Can utterly abolish or destroy!
  Hence, in a season of calm weather
      Though inland far we be,
Our souls have sight of that immortal sea
    Which brought us hither;
    Can in a moment travel thither—
And see the children sport upon the shore,
And hear the mighty waters rolling evermore.

Then, sing ye birds, sing, sing a joyous song!
     And let the young lambs bound
     As to the tabor's sound!
  We, in thought, will join your throng
     Ye that pipe and ye that play,
     Ye that through your hearts to-day
     Feel the gladness of the May!
What though the radiance which was once so bright
Be now for ever taken from my sight,
  Though nothing can bring back the hour
Of splendour in the grass, of glory in the flower;
    We will grieve not, rather find
    Strength in what remains behind;
    In the primal sympathy
    Which having been must ever be;

        In the soothing thoughts that spring
        Out of human suffering;
        In the faith that looks through death,
In years that bring the philosophic mind.

And O, ye Fountains, Meadows, Hills and Groves,
Forebode not any severing of our loves!
Yet in my heart of hearts I feel your might;
I only have relinquish'd one delight
To live beneath your more habitual sway;
I love the brooks which down their channels fret
Even more than when I tripp'd lightly as they;
The innocent brightness of a new-born day
        Is lovely yet;
The clouds that gather round the setting sun
Do take a sober colouring from an eye
That hath kept watch o'er man's mortality;
Another race hath been, and other palms are won.
Thanks to the human heart by which we live,
Thanks to its tenderness, its joys, and fears,
To me the meanest flower that blows can give
Thoughts that do often lie too deep for tears.

SAMUEL TAYLOR COLERIDGE
(1772-1834)

DEJECTION: AN ODE

WRITTEN APRIL 4, 1802.

Late, late yestreen I saw the new moon,
With the old moon in her arms;
And I fear, I fear, my Master dear!
We shall have a deadly storm.
Ballad of Sir Patrick Spence.

I

WELL! If the Bard was weather-wise, who made
  The grand old ballad of Sir Patrick Spence,
  This night, so tranquil now, will not go hence
Unroused by winds, that ply a busier trade
Than those which mould yon cloud in lazy flakes,
Or the dull sobbing draft, that moans and rakes
  Upon the strings of this Æolian lute,
  Which better far were mute.
For lo! the New-moon winter-bright!
And overspread with phantom light,
(With swimming phantom light o'erspread
But rimmed and circled by a silver thread)
I see the old Moon in her lap, foretelling
  The coming-on of rain and squally blast.
And oh! that even now the gust were swelling,
  And the slant night-shower driving loud and fast!
Those sounds which oft have raised me, whilst they awed,
    And sent my soul abroad,
Might now perhaps their wonted impulse give,
Might startle this dull pain, and make it move and live!

II

A grief without a pang, void, dark, and drear,
  A stifled, drowsy, unimpassioned grief,
  Which finds no natural outlet, no relief,
    In word, or sigh, or tear—
O Lady! in this wan and heartless mood,
To other thoughts by yonder throstle woo'd,
  All this long eve, so balmy and serene,
Have I been gazing on the western sky,
  And its peculiar tint of yellow green:
And still I gaze—and with how blank an eye!
And those thin clouds above, in flakes and bars,
That give away their motion to the stars;
Those stars, that glide behind them or between,
Now sparkling, now bedimmed, but always seen:
Yon crescent Moon, as fixed as if it grew
In its own cloudless, starless lake of blue;
I see them all so excellently fair,
I see, not feel, how beautiful they are!

III

  My genial spirits fail;
  And what can these avail
To lift the smothering weight from off my breast?
  It were a vain endeavour,
  Though I should gaze for ever
On that green light that lingers in the west:
I may not hope from outward forms to win
The passions and the life, whose fountains are within.

IV

O Lady! we receive but what we give,
And in our life alone does Nature live:

Ours is her wedding-garment, ours her shroud!
   And would we aught behold, of higher worth,
Than that inanimate cold world allowed
To the poor loveless ever-anxious crowd,
   Ah! from the soul itself must issue forth
A light, a glory, a fair luminous cloud
      Enveloping the Earth—
And from the soul itself must there be sent
   A sweet and potent voice, of its own birth,
Of all sweet sounds the life and element!

V

O pure of heart! thou need'st not ask of me
What this strong music in the soul may be!
What, and wherein it doth exist,
This light, this glory, this fair luminous mist,
This beautiful and beauty-making power.
   Joy, virtuous Lady! Joy that ne'er was given,
Save to the pure, and in their purest hour,
Life, and Life's effluence, cloud at once and shower,
Joy, Lady! is the spirit and the power,
Which wedding Nature to us gives in dower,
   A new Earth and new Heaven,
Undreamt of by the sensual and the proud—
Joy is the sweet voice, Joy the luminous cloud—
     We in ourselves rejoice!
And thence flows all that charms or ear or sight,
   All melodies the echoes of that voice,
All colours a suffusion from that light.

VI

There was a time when, though my path was rough,
   This joy within me dallied with distress,

And all misfortunes were but as the stuff
   Whence Fancy made me dreams of happiness:
For Hope grew round me, like the twining vine,
And fruits, and foliage, not my own, seemed mine.
But now afflictions bow me down to earth;
Nor care I that they rob me of my mirth;
     But Oh! each visitation
Suspends what Nature gave me at my birth,
   My shaping spirit of Imagination.
For not to think of what I needs must feel,
   But to be still and patient, all I can;
And haply by abstruse research to steal
   From my own nature all the natural man—
   This was my sole resource, my only plan:
Till that which suits a part infects the whole,
And now is almost grown the habit of my soul.

VII

Hence, viper thoughts, that coil around my mind,
     Reality's dark dream!
I turn from you, and listen to the wind,
   Which long has raved unnoticed. What a scream
Of agony by torture lengthened out
That lute sent forth! Thou Wind, that rav'st without,
   Bare crag, or mountain-tairn, or blasted tree,
Or pine-grove whither woodman never clomb,
Or lonely house, long held the witches' home,
   Methinks were fitter instruments for thee,
Mad Lutanist! who in this month of showers,
Of dark-brown gardens, and of peeping flowers,
Mak'st Devil's yule, with worse than wintry song,
The blossoms, buds, and timorous leaves among.

Thou actor, perfect in all tragic sounds!
Thou mighty Poet, even to frenzy bold!
 What tell'st thou now about?
 'Tis of the rushing of an host in rout,
With groans of trampled man, with smarting wounds—
At once they groan with pain, and shudder with the cold!
But hush! there is a pause of deepest silence!
 And all that noise, as of a rushing crowd,
With groans, and tremulous shudderings—all is over—
 It tells another tale, with sounds less deep and loud!
  A tale of less affright,
  And tempered with delight,
As Otway's self had framed the tender lay,
  'Tis of a little child
  Upon a lonesome wild,
Not far from home, but she hath lost her way:
And now moans low in bitter grief and fear,
And now screams loud, and hopes to make her mother hear.

VIII

'Tis midnight, but small thoughts have I of sleep:
Full seldom may my friend such vigils keep!
Visit her, gentle Sleep! with wings of healing,
 And may this storm be but a mountain-birth,
May all the stars hang bright above her dwelling,
 Silent as though they watched the sleeping Earth!
  With light heart may she rise,
  Gay fancy, cheerful eyes,
 Joy lift her spirit, joy attune her voice;
To her may all things live, from pole to pole,

Their life the eddying of her living soul!
O simple spirit, guided from above,
Dear Lady, friend devoutest of my choice,
Thus mayest thou ever, evermore rejoice.

WALTER SAVAGE LANDOR (1775–1864)

TO WORDSWORTH

THOSE who have laid the harp aside
  And turn'd to idler things,
From very restlessness have tried
  The loose and dusty strings,
And, catching back some favourite strain,
Run with it o'er the chords again.

But Memory is not a Muse,
  O Wordsworth! though 'tis said
They all descend from her, and use
  To haunt her fountain-head:
That other men should work for me
In the rich mines of Poesie,

Pleases me better than the toil
  Of smoothing under hardened hand,
With Attic emery and oil,
  The shining point for Wisdom's wand,
Like those thou temperest 'mid the rills
Descending from thy native hills.

Without his governance, in vain
  Manhood is strong, and Youth is bold.

If oftentimes the o'er-piled strain
　　Clogs in the furnace, and grows cold
Beneath his pinions deep and frore,
And swells and melts and flows no more,

That is because the heat beneath
　　Pants in its cavern poorly fed,
Life springs not from the couch of Death,
　　Nor Muse nor Grace can raise the dead;
Unturn'd then let the mass remain,
Intractable to sun or rain.

A marsh, where only flat leaves lie,
And showing but the broken sky,
Too surely is the sweetest lay
That wins the ear and wastes the day,
Where youthful Fancy pouts alone
And lets not Wisdom touch her zone.

He who would build his fame up high,
The rule and plummet must apply,
Nor say, "I'll do what I have plann'd,"
Before he try if loam or sand
Be still remaining in the place
Delved for each polisht pillar's base.
With skilful eye and fit device
Thou raisest every edifice,
Whether in sheltered vale it stand
Or overlook the Dardan strand,
Amid the cypresses that mourn
Laodameia's love forlorn.

We both have run o'er half the space
Listed for mortal's earthly race;

We both have crost life's fervid line,
And other stars before us shine:
May they be bright and prosperous
As those that have been stars for us!
Our course by Milton's light was sped,
And Shakespeare shining overhead:
Chatting on deck was Dryden too,
The Bacon of the rhyming crew;
None ever crost our mystic sea
More richly stored with thought than he:
Tho' never tender nor sublime,
He wrestles with and conquers Time.
To learn my lore on Chaucer's knee,
I left much prouder company;
Thee gentle Spenser fondly led,
But me he mostly sent to bed.
I wish them every joy above
That highly blessed spirits prove,
Save one; and that too shall be theirs,
But after many rolling years,
When 'mid their light thy light appears.

GEORGE GORDON NOEL LORD BYRON (1788–1824)

ODE ON VENICE

I

Oh Venice! Venice! when thy marble walls
Are level with the waters, there shall be
A cry of nations o'er thy sunken halls,
A loud lament along the sweeping sea!
If I, a northern wanderer, weep for thee,
What should thy sons do?—anything but weep:
And yet they only murmur in their sleep.
In contrast with their fathers—as the slime,
The dull green ooze of the receding deep,
Is with the dashing of the spring-tide foam,
That drives the sailor shipless to his home,
Are they to those that were; and thus they creep,
Crouching and crab-like, through their sapping streets.
Oh! agony—that centuries should reap
No mellower harvest! Thirteen hundred years
Of wealth and glory turn'd to dust and tears;
And every monument the stranger meets,
Church, palace, pillar, as a mourner greets;
And even the Lion all subdued appears,
And the harsh sound of the barbarian drum,
With dull and daily dissonance, repeats
The echo of thy tyrant's voice along
The soft waves, once all musical to song,

Ode on Venice. The ode was transmitted from Venice, along with the poem entitled *Mazeppa.*

That heaved beneath the moonlight with the throng
Of gondolas—and to the busy hum
Of cheerful creatures, whose most sinful deeds
Were but the overbeating of the heart,
And flow of too much happiness, which needs
The aid of age to turn its course apart
From the luxuriant and voluptuous flood
Of sweet sensations, battling with the blood.
But these are better than the gloomy errors,
The weeds of nations in their last decay,
When Vice walks forth with her unsoften'd terrors,
And Mirth is madness, and but smiles to slay;
And Hope is nohing but a false delay,
The sick man's lightning half an hour ere death,
When Faintness, the last mortal birth of Pain,
And apathy of limb, the dull beginning
Of the cold staggering race which Death is winning,
Steals vein by vein and pulse by pulse away;
Yet so relieving the o'er-tortured clay,
To him appears renewal of his breath,
And freedom the mere numbness of his chain;—
And then he talks of life, and how again
He feels his spirits soaring—albeit weak,
And of the fresher air, which he would seek;
And as he whispers knows not that he gasps,
That his thin finger feels not what it clasps,
And so the film comes o'er him, and the dizzy
Chamber swims round and round, and shadows busy,
At which he vainly catches, flit and gleam,
Till the last rattle chokes the strangled scream,
And all is ice and blackness,—and the earth
That which it was the moment ere our birth.

II

There is no hope for nations!—Search the page
Of many thousand years—the daily scene,
The flow and ebb of each recurring age,
The everlasting *to be* which *hath been*,
Hath taught us naught or little: still we lean
On things that rot beneath our weight, and wear
Our strength away in wrestling with the air;
For 'tis our nature strikes us down: the beasts
Slaughter'd in hourly hecatombs for feasts
Are of as high an order—they must go
Even where their driver goads them, though to slaughter.
Ye men, who pour your blood for kings as water,
What have they given your children in return?
A heritage of servitude and woes,
A blindfold bondage, where your hire is blows.
What! do not yet the red-hot ploughshares burn,
O'er which you stumble in a false ideal,
And deem this proof of loyalty the *real*;
Kissing the hand that guides you to your scars,
And glorying as you tread the glowing bars?
All that your sires have left you, all that Time
Bequeaths of free, and History of sublime,
Spring from a different theme! Ye see and read,
Admire and sigh, and then succumb and bleed!
Save the few spirits, who despite of all,
And worse than all, the sudden crimes engender'd
By the down-thundering of the prison wall,
And thirst to swallow the sweet waters tender'd,
Gushing from Freedom's fountain—when the crowd,
Madden'd with centuries of drought, are loud,
And trample on each other to obtain

The cup which brings oblivion of a chain
Heavy and sore,—in which long yoked they plough'd
The sand—or if there sprung the yellow grain,
'Twas not for them, their necks were too much bow'd,
And their dead palates chew'd the cud of pain:—
Yes! the few spirits—who, despite of deeds
Which they abhor, confound not with the cause
Those momentary starts from Nature's laws,
Which, like the pestilence and earthquake, smite
But for a term, then pass, and leave the earth
With all her seasons to repair the blight
With a few summers, and again put forth
Cities and generations—fair, when free—
For, Tyranny, there blooms no bud for thee!

III

Glory and Empire! once upon these towers
With freedom—godlike Triad! how ye sate!
The league of mightiest nations, in those hours
When Venice was an envy, might abate,
But did not quench, her spirit; in her fate
All were enwrapp'd; the feasted monarchs knew
And loved their hostess, nor could learn to hate,
Although they humbled—with the kingly few
The many felt, for from all days and climes
She was the voyager's worship; even her crimes
Were of the softer order—born of Love,
She drank no blood, nor fatten'd on the dead,
But gladden'd where her harmless conquests spread;
For these restored the Cross, that from above
Hallow'd her sheltering banners, which incessant
Flew between earth and the unholy Crescent,
Which, if it waned and dwindled, Earth may thank

The city it has clothed in chains, which clank
Now, creaking in the ears of those who owe
The name of Freedom to her glorious struggles;
Yet she but shares with them a common woe,
And call'd the "kingdom" of a conquering foe,—
But knows what all—and, most of all, *we* know—
With what set gilded terms a tyrant juggles!

IV

The name of Commonwealth is past and gone
O'er the three fractions of the groaning globe;
Venice is crush'd, and Holland deigns to own
A sceptre, and endures the purple robe;
If the free Switzer yet bestrides alone
His chainless mountains, 'tis but for a time,
For tyranny of late is cunning grown,
And in its own good season tramples down
The sparkles of our ashes. One great clime,
Whose vigorous offspring by dividing ocean
Are kept apart and nursed in the devotion
Of Freedom, which their fathers fought for, and
Bequeath'd—a heritage of heart and hand,
And proud distinction from each other land,
Whose sons must bow them at a monarch's motion,
As if his senseless sceptre were a wand
Full of the magic of exploded science—
Still one great clime, in full and free defiance,
Yet rears her crest, unconquer'd and sublime,
Above the far Atlantic!—She has taught
Her Esau-brethren that the haughty flag,
The floating fence of Albion's feebler crag,
May strike to those whose red right hands have bought
Rights cheaply earn'd with blood.—Still, still, for ever

Better, though each man's life-blood were a river,
That it should flow, and overflow, than creep
Through thousand lazy channels in our veins,
Damm'd like the dull canal with locks and chains,
And moving, as a sick man in his sleep,
Three paces, and then faltering:—better be
Where the extinguish'd Spartans still are free,
In their proud charnel of Thermopylæ,
Than stagnate in our marsh,—or o'er the deep
Fly, and one current to the ocean add,
One spirit to the souls our fathers had,
One freeman more, America, to thee!

PERCY BYSSHE SHELLEY (1792–1822)

TO LIBERTY

I

A GLORIOUS people vibrated again
  The lightning of the nations: Liberty
From heart to heart, from tower to tower, o'er Spain,
  Scattering contagious fire into the sky,
Gleamed. My soul spurned the chains of its dismay,
    And in the rapid plumes of song
    Clothed itself, sublime and strong,
(As a young eagle soars the morning clouds among),
    Hovering in verse o'er its accustomed prey;
    Till from its station in the Heaven of fame
  The Spirit's whirlwind rapt it, and the ray
    Of the remotest sphere of living flame
Which paves the void was from behind it flung,
  As foam from a ship's swiftness, when there came
  A voice out of the deep: I will record the same.

II

"The Sun and the serenest moon sprang forth:
   The burning stars of the abyss were hurled
Into the depths of Heaven. The dædal earth,
   That island in the ocean of the world,
   Hung in its cloud of all-sustaining air:
      But this divinest universe
      Was yet a chaos and a curse,
For thou wert not; but, power from worst producing worse,
   The spirit of the beasts was kindled there,
     And of the birds, and of the watery forms,
And there was war among them, and despair
     Within them, raging without truce or terms:
The bosom of their violated nurse
   Groaned, for beasts warred on beasts, and worms on worms,
And men on men; each heart was as a hell of storms.

III

"Man, the imperial shape, then multiplied
   His generations under the pavilion
Of the Sun's throne: palace and pyramid,
   Temple and prison, to many a swarming million
Were, as to mountain-wolves their ragged caves.
      This human living multitude
      Was savage, cunning, blind, and rude,
For thou wert not; but o'er the populous solitude,
   Like one fierce cloud over a waste of waves,
     Hung Tyranny; beneath, sate deified
   The sister-pest, congregator of slaves;
      Into the shadow of her pinions wide

Anarchs and priests, who feed on gold and blood
  Till with the stain their inmost souls are dyed,
  Drove the astonished herds of men from every side.

IV

"The nodding promontories, and blue isles,
  And cloud-like mountains, and dividuous waves
Of Greece, basked glorious in the open smiles
  Of favouring Heaven: from their enchanted caves
Prophetic echoes flung dim melody,
    On the unapprehensive wild,
    The vine, the corn, the olive mild,
Grew savage yet, to human use unreconciled;
  And, like unfolded flowers beneath the sea,
    Like the man's thought dark in the infant's brain,
  Like aught that is which wraps what is to be,
    Art's deathless dreams lay veiled by many a vein
Of Parian stone; and, yet a speechless child,
  Verse murmured, and Philosophy did strain
  Her lidless eyes for thee; when o'er the Ægean main

V

"Athens arose; a city such as vision
  Builds from the purple crags and silver towers
Of battlemented cloud, as in derision
  Of kingliest masonry; the ocean-floors
Pave it; the evening sky pavilions it;
    Its portals are inhabited
    By thunder-zonéd winds, each head
Within its cloudy wings with sun-fire garlanded,—
  A divine work! Athens, diviner yet,
    Gleamed with its crest of columns, on the will
  Of man, as on a mount of diamond, set;

For thou wert, and thine all-creative skill
Peopled, with forms that mock the eternal dead
In marble immortality, that hill
Which was thine earliest throne and latest oracle.

VI

"Within the surface of Time's fleeting river
　Its wrinkled image lies, as then it lay
Immovably unquiet, and for ever
　It trembles, but it cannot pass away!
The voices of thy bards and sages thunder
　　With an earth-awakening blast
　　Through the caverns of the past:
Religion veils her eyes; Oppression sinks aghast;
　A wingéd sound of joy, and love, and wonder,
　　Which soars where Expectation never flew,
　Rending the veil of space and time asunder!
　　One ocean feeds the clouds, and streams, and dew;
One Sun illumines Heaven; One Spirit vast
　With life and love makes chaos ever new,
　As Athens doth the world with thy delight renew.

VII

"Then Rome was, and from thy deep bosom fairest
　Like a wolf-cub from a Cadmæan Mænad,
She drew the milk of greatness, though thy dearest
　From that Elysian food was yet unweanéd;
And many a deed of terrible uprightness
　　By thy sweet love was sanctified;
　　And in thy smile, and by thy side,
Saintly Camillus lived, and firm Atilius died.

    But when tears stained thy robe of vestal whiteness,
        And gold profaned thy Capitolian throne,
  Thou didst desert, with spirit-wingéd lightness,
        The senate of the tyrants; they sunk prone
Slaves of one tyrant: Palatinus sighed
        Faint echoes of Ionian song; that tone
        Thou didst delay to hear, lamenting to disown.

VIII

"From what Hyrcanian glen or frozen hill,
    Or piny promontory of the Arctic main,
Or utmost islet inaccessible,
    Didst thou lament the ruin of thy reign,
Teaching the woods and waves, and desert rocks,
        And every Naiad's ice-cold urn,
        To talk in echoes sad and stern
Of that sublimest love which man had dared unlearn?
    For neither didst thou watch the wizard flocks
        Of the Scald's dreams, nor haunt the Druid's sleep.
    What if the tears rained through thy scattered locks
        Were quickly dried? for thou didst groan, not weep,
When from the sea of death, to kill and burn,
    The Galilean serpent forth did creep,
    And made thy world an undistinguishable heap.

IX

"A thousand years the earth cried, 'Where art thou?'
    And then the shadow of thy coming fell
On Saxon Alfred's olive-cinctured brow;
    And many a warrior-peopled citadel,
Like rocks which fire lifts out of the flat deep,
        Arose in sacred Italy,
        Frowning o'er the tempestuous sea

Of kings, and priests, and slaves, in tower-crowned
    majesty;
  That multitudinous anarchy did sweep
    And burst around their walls, like idle foam,
  Whilst from the human spirit's deepest deep
    Strange melody with love and awe struck dumb
Dissonant arms; and Art, which cannot die,
  With divine wand traced on our earthly home
  Fit imagery to pave Heaven's everlasting dome.

X

"Thou huntress swifter than the Moon! thou terror
  Of the world's wolves! thou bearer of the quiver,
Whose sunlike shafts pierce tempest-wingèd Error,
  As light may pierce the clouds when they dissever
In the calm regions of the orient day!
    Luther caught thy wakening glance;
    Like lightning, from his leaden lance
Reflected, it dissolved the visions of the trance
  In which, as in a tomb, the nations lay;
    And England's prophets hailed thee as their queen,
  In songs whose music cannot pass away,
    Though it must flow for ever: not unseen
Before the spirit-sighted countenance
  Of Milton didst thou pass, from the sad scene
  Beyond whose night he saw, with a dejected mien.

XI

"The eager hours and unreluctant years
  As on a dawn-illumined mountain stood,
Trampling to silence their loud hopes and fears,
  Darkening each other with their multitude,

And cried aloud, 'Liberty!' Indignation
    Answered Pity from her cave;
    Death grew pale within the grave,
And Desolation howled to the destroyer, Save!
  When like Heaven's Sun girt by the exhalation
    Of its own glorious light, thou didst arise,
  Chasing thy foes from nation unto nation
    Like shadows: as if day had cloven the skies
At dreaming midnight o'er the western wave,
  Men started, staggering with a glad surprise,
  Under the lightnings of thine unfamiliar eyes.

XII

"Thou heaven of earth! what spells could pall thee then
    In ominous eclipse? a thousand years
Bred from the slime of deep Oppression's den,
    Dyed all thy liquid light with blood and tears,
Till thy sweet stars could weep the stain away;
    How like Bacchanals of blood
    Round France, the ghastly vintage, stood
Destruction's sceptred slaves, and Folly's mitred brood!
  When one, like them, but mightier far than they,
    The Anarch of thine own bewildered powers,
  Rose: armies mingled in obscure array,
    Like clouds with clouds, darkening the sacred bowers
Of serene Heaven. He, by the past pursued,
  Rests with those dead, but unforgotten hours,
  Whose ghosts scare victor kings in their ancestral
    towers.

XIII

"England yet sleeps: was she not called of old?
  Spain calls her now, as with its thrilling thunder

Vesuvius wakens Ætna, and the cold
  Snow-crags by its reply are cloven in sunder:
O'er the lit waves every Æolian isle
    From Pithecusa to Pelorus
    Howls, and leaps, and glares in chorus:
They cry, 'Be dim, ye lamps of Heaven suspended o'er us!'
  Her chains are threads of gold, she need but smile
    And they dissolve; but Spain's were links of steel
  Till bit to dust by virtue's keenest file.
    Twins of a single destiny! appeal
To the eternal years enthroned before us
  In the dim West; impress as from a seal,
  All ye have thought and done! Time cannot dare conceal.

XIV

"Tomb of Arminius! render up thy dead
  Till, like a standard from a watch-tower's staff,
His soul may stream over the tyrant's head;
  Thy victory shall be his epitaph,
Wild Bacchanal of truth's mysterious wine,
    King-deluded Germany,
    His dead spirit lives in thee.
Why do we fear or hope? thou art already free!
  And thou, lost Paradise of this divine
    And glorious world! thou flowery wilderness!
  Thou island of eternity! thou shrine
    Where Desolation, clothed with loveliness,
Worships the thing thou wert! O Italy,
  Gather thy blood into thy heart; repress
  The beasts who make their dens thy sacred palaces.

XV

"Oh, that the free would stamp the impious name
  Of KING into the dust! or write it there,
So that this blot upon the page of fame
  Were as a serpent's path, which the light air
Erases, and the flat sands close behind!
    Ye the oracle have heard:
    Lift the victory-flashing sword,
And cut the snaky knots of this foul Gordian word,
    Which, weak itself as stubble, yet can bind
      Into a mass, irrefragably firm,
    The axes and the rods which awe mankind;
      The sound has poison in it, 'tis the sperm
Of what makes life foul, cankerous, and abhorred;
    Disdain not thou, at thine appointed term,
    To set thine arméd heel on this reluctant worm.

XVI

"Oh, that the wise from their bright minds would kindle
  Such lamps within the dome of this dim world,
That the pale name of PRIEST might shrink and dwindle
  Into the hell from which it first was hurled,
A scoff of impious pride from fiends impure;
    Till human thoughts might kneel alone,
    Each before the judgment-throne
Of its own aweless soul, or of the Power unknown!
    Oh, that the words which make the thoughts obscure
      From which they spring, as clouds of glimmering dew
    From a white lake blot Heaven's blue portraiture,
      Were stripped of their thin masks and various hue
And frowns and smiles and splendours not their own,
    Till in the nakedness of false and true
    They stand before their Lord, each to receive its due!

XVII

"He who taught man to vanquish whatsoever
  Can be between the cradle and the grave
Crowned him the King of Life. Oh, vain endeavour!
  If on his own high will, a willing slave
He has enthroned the oppression and the oppressor.
    What if earth can clothe and feed
    Amplest millions at their need,
And power in thought be as the tree within the seed?
  Or what if Art, an ardent intercessor,
    Driving on fiery wings to Nature's throne,
  Checks the great mother stooping to caress her
    And cries: 'Give me, thy child, dominion
Over all height and depth'? if Life can breed
  New wants, and wealth from those who toil and groan
Rend of thy gifts and hers a thousandfold for one!

XVIII

"Come thou, but lead out of the inmost cave
  Of man's deep spirit, as the morning-star
Beckons the Sun from the Eoan wave,
  Wisdom. I hear the pennons of her car
Self-moving, like cloud charioted by flame;
    Comes she not, and come ye not,
    Rulers of eternal thought,
To judge, with solemn truth, life's ill-apportioned lot?
  Blind Love, and equal Justice, and the Fame
    Of what has been, the Hope of what will be?
  O Liberty! if such could be thy name
    Wert thou disjoined from these, or they from thee;

If thine or theirs were treasures to be bought
  By blood or tears, have not the wise and free
  Wept tears, and blood like tears?"—The solemn harmony

XIX

Paused, and the Spirit of that mighty singing
  To its abyss was suddenly withdrawn;
Then, as a wild swan, when sublimely winging
  Its path athwart the thunder-smoke of dawn,
Sinks headlong through the aërial golden light
    On the heavy sounding plain,
    When the bolt has pierced its brain;
As summer clouds dissolve, unburthened of their rain;
  As a far taper fades with fading night,
    As a brief insect dies with dying day—
My song, its pinions disarrayed of might,
    Drooped; o'er it closed the echoes far away
Of the great voice which did its flight sustain,
  As waves which lately paved his watery way
  Hiss round a drowner's head in their tempestuous play.

ODE TO THE WEST WIND

O WILD West Wind, thou breath of Autumn's being,
Thou, from whose unseen presence the leaves dead
Are driven, like ghosts from an enchanter fleeing,
Yellow, and black, and pale, and hectic red,
Pestilence-stricken multitudes: O thou
Who chariotest to their dark wintry bed
The wingéd seeds, where they lie cold and low,

Each like a corpse within its grave, until
Thine azure sister of the Spring shall blow
Her clarion o'er the dreaming earth, and fill
(Driving sweet buds like flocks to feed in air)
With living hues and odours plain and hill:
Wild Spirit, which art moving everywhere;
Destroyer and Preserver; Hear, oh, hear!

Thou on whose stream, 'mid the steep sky's commotion,
Loose clouds like earth's decaying leaves are shed,
Shook from the tangled boughs of Heaven and Ocean,
Angels of rain and lightning; there are spread
On the blue surface of thine airy surge,
Like the bright hair uplifted from the head
Of some fierce Mænad, ev'n from the dim verge
Of the horizon to the zenith's height—
The locks of the approaching storm. Thou dirge
Of the dying year, to which this closing night
Will be the dome of a vast sepulchre,
Vaulted with all thy congregated might
Of vapours, from whose solid atmosphere
Black rain, and fire, and hail, will burst: oh, hear!

Thou who didst waken from his summer-dreams,
The blue Mediterranean, where he lay,
Lull'd by the coil of his crystalline streams,
Beside a pumice isle in Baiæ's bay,
And saw in sleep old palaces and towers
Quivering within the wave's intenser day,
All overgrown with azure moss and flowers
So sweet, the sense faints picturing them! Thou
For whose path the Atlantic's level powers
Cleave themselves into chasms, while far below

The sea-blooms and the oozy woods which wear
The sapless foliage of the ocean, know
Thy voice, and suddenly grow grey with fear
And tremble and despoil themselves: oh, hear!

If I were a dead leaf thou mightest bear;
If I were a swift cloud to fly with thee;
A wave to pant beneath thy power, and share
The impulse of thy strength, only less free
Than Thou, O uncontrollable! If even
I were as in my boyhood, and could be
The comrade of thy wanderings over heaven,
As then, when to outstrip thy skyey speed
Scarce seem'd a vision, I would ne'er have striven
As thus with thee in prayer in my sore need.
Oh, lift me as a wave, a leaf, a cloud!
I fall upon the thorns of life! I bleed!
A heavy weight of hours has chain'd and bow'd
One too like thee: tameless, and swift, and proud.

Make me thy lyre, ev'n as the forest is:
What if my leaves are falling like its own!
The tumult of thy mighty harmonies
Will take from both a deep autumnal tone,
Sweet though in sadness. Be thou, Spirit fierce,
My spirit! be thou me, impetuous one!
Drive my dead thoughts over the universe
Like wither'd leaves to quicken a new birth;
And, by the incantation of this verse,
Scatter, as from an unextinguish'd hearth
Ashes and sparks, my words among mankind!
Be through my lips to unawaken'd earth
The trumpet of a prophecy! O Wind,
If Winter comes, can Spring be far behind?

TO A SKYLARK

Hail to thee, blithe Spirit!
  Bird thou never wert,
That from heaven, or near it
  Pourest thy full heart
In profuse strains of unpremeditated art.

Higher still and higher
  From the earth thou springest
Like a cloud of fire;
  The blue deep thou wingest,
And singing still dost soar, and soaring ever singest.

In the golden lightning
  Of the sunken sun
O'er which clouds are brightening,
  Thou dost float and run,
Like an unbodied joy whose race is just begun.

The pale purple even
  Melts around thy flight;
Like a star of heaven
  In the broad daylight
Thou art unseen, but yet I hear thy shrill delight:

Keen as are the arrows
  Of that silver sphere,
Whose intense lamp narrows
  In the white dawn clear
Until we hardly see, we feel that it is there.

All the earth and air
  With thy voice is loud,
As, when night is bare,
  From one lonely cloud
The moon rains out her beams, and heaven is overflow'd.

What thou art we know not;
  What is most like thee?
From rainbow clouds there flow not
  Drops so bright to see
As from thy presence showers a rain of melody.

Like a poet hidden
  In the light of thought,
Singing hymns unbidden,
  Till the world is wrought
To sympathy with hopes and fears it heeded not:

Like a high-born maiden
  In a palace tower,
Soothing her love-laden
  Soul in secret hour
With music sweet as love, which overflows her bower:

Like a glow-worm golden
  In a dell of dew,
Scattering unbeholden
  Its aërial hue
Among the flowers and grass, which screen it from the view:

Like a rose embower'd
  In its own green leaves,
By warm winds deflower'd,
  Till the scent it gives
Makes faint with too much sweet these heavy-wingéd thieves.

Sound of vernal showers
  On the twinkling grass,
Rain-awaken'd flowers,
  All that ever was
Joyous, and clear, and fresh, thy music doth surpass.

Teach us, sprite or bird,
  What sweet thoughts are thine:
I have never heard
  Praise of love or wine
That panted forth a flood of rapture so divine.

Chorus hymeneal
  Or triumphal chaunt
Match'd with thine, would be all
  But an empty vaunt—
A thing wherein we feel there is some hidden want.

What objects are the fountains
  Of thy happy strain?
What fields, or waves, or mountains?
  What shapes of sky or plain?
What love of thine own kind? what ignorance of pain?

With thy clear keen joyance
  Languor cannot be:
Shadow of annoyance
  Never came near thee:
Thou lovest; but ne'er knew love's sad satiety.

Waking or asleep
   Thou of death must deem
Things more true and deep
   Than we mortals dream,
Or how could thy notes flow in such a crystal stream?

We look before and after,
   And pine for what is not:
Our sincerest laughter
   With some pain is fraught;
Our sweetest songs are those that tell of saddest thought.

Yet if we could scorn
   Hate, and pride, and fear;
If we were things born
   Not to shed a tear,
I know not how thy joy we ever should come near.

Better than all measures
   Of delightful sound,
Better than all treasures
   That in books are found,
Thy skill to poet were, thou scorner of the ground!

Teach me half the gladness
   That thy brain must know,
Such harmonious madness
   From my lips would flow
The world should listen then, as I am listening now!

JOHN KEATS (1795–1821)

ON A GRECIAN URN

Thou still unravish'd bride of quietness,
  Thou foster-child of Silence and slow Time,
Sylvan historian, who canst thus express
  A flowery tale more sweetly than our rhyme:
What leaf-fringed legend haunts about thy shape
  Of deities or mortals, or of both,
    In Tempe or the dales of Arcady?
What men or gods are these? What maidens loath?
What mad pursuit? What struggle to escape?
  What pipes and timbrels? What wild ecstasy?

Heard melodies are sweet, but those unheard
  Are sweeter; therefore, ye soft pipes, play on;
Not to the sensual ear, but, more endear'd,
  Pipe to the spirit ditties of no tone;
Fair youth, beneath the trees, thou canst not leave
  Thy song, nor ever can those trees be bare;
    Bold lover, never, never canst thou kiss,
Though winning near the goal—yet, do not grieve;
    She cannot fade, though thou hast not thy bliss,
For ever wilt thou love, and she be fair!

Ah, happy, happy boughs! that cannot shed
  Your leaves, nor ever bid the Spring adieu;
And, happy melodist, unwearied,
  For ever piping songs for ever new;
More happy love! more happy, happy love!

For ever warm and still to be enjoy'd,
    For ever panting and for ever young;
All breathing human passion far above,
    That leaves a heart high-sorrowful and cloyed,
        A burning forehead, and a parching tongue.

Who are these coming to the sacrifice?
    To what green altar, O mysterious priest,
Lead'st thou that heifer lowing at the skies,
    And all her silken flanks with garlands drest?
What little town by river or sea-shore,
    Or mountain-built with peaceful citadel,
        Is emptied of its folk, this pious morn?
And, little town, thy streets for evermore
    Will silent be; and not a soul to tell
        Why thou art desolate, can e'er return.

O Attic shape! Fair attitude! with brede
    Of marble men and maidens overwrought,
With forest branches and the trodden weed;
    Thou silent form! dost tease us out of thought
As doth eternity: Cold Pastoral!
    When old age shall this generation waste,
        Thou shalt remain, in midst of other woe
    Than ours, a friend to man, to whom thou say'st,
"Beauty is truth, truth beauty,"—that is all
    Ye know on earth, and all ye need to know.

ODE TO A NIGHTINGALE

My heart aches, and a drowsy numbness pains
   My sense, as though of hemlock I had drunk,
Or emptied some dull opiate to the drains
   One minute past, and Lethe-wards had sunk:
'Tis not through envy of thy happy lot,
   But being too happy in thy happiness—
     That thou, light-wingéd Dryad of the trees,
        In some melodious plot
Of beechen green, and shadows numberless,
   Singest of summer in full-throated ease.

O for a draught of vintage; that hath been
   Cool'd a long age in the deep-delvéd earth,
Tasting of Flora and the country green,
   Dance, and Provençal song, and sun-burnt mirth!
O for a beaker full of the warm South,
   Full of the true, the blushful Hippocrene,
     With beaded bubbles winking at the brim
        And purple-stainéd mouth;
That I might drink, and leave the world unseen,
   And with thee fade away into the forest dim:

Fade far away, dissolve, and quite forget
   What thou among the leaves hast never known,
The weariness, the fever, and the fret
   Here, where men sit and hear each other groan;
Where palsy shakes a few, sad, last grey hairs,
   Where you thgrows pale, and spectre-thin, and dies;
     Where but to think is to be full of sorrow
        And leaden-eyed despairs;
Where Beauty cannot keep her lustrous eyes,
   Or new Love pine at them beyond to-morrow.

Away! away! for I will fly to thee,
　Not charioted by Bacchus and his pards,
But on the viewless wings of Poesy,
　Though the dull brain perplexes and retards:
Already with thee! tender is the night,
　And haply the Queen-Moon is on her throne,
　　Cluster'd around by all her starry Fays;
　　　But here there is no light
　Save what from heaven is with the breezes blown
　　Through verdurous glooms and winding mossy ways.

I cannot see what flowers are at my feet,
　Nor what soft incense hangs upon the boughs,
But, in embalmèd darkness, guess each sweet
　Wherewith the seasonable month endows
The grass, the thicket, and the fruit-tree wild;
　White hawthorn, and the pastoral eglantine;
　　Fast-fading violets cover'd up in leaves;
　　　And mid-May's eldest child
　The coming musk-rose, full of dewy wine,
　　The murmurous haunt of flies on summer eves.

Darkling I listen; and for many a time
　I have been half in love with easeful Death,
Call'd him soft names in many a musèd rhyme,
　To take into the air my quiet breath;
Now more than ever seems it rich to die,
　To cease upon the midnight with no pain,
　　While thou art pouring forth thy soul abroad
　　　In such an ecstasy!
　Still wouldst thou sing, and I have ears in vain—
　　To thy high requiem become a sod.

Thou wast not born for death, immortal Bird!
  No hungry generations tread thee down!
The voice I hear this passing night was heard
  In ancient days by emperor and clown:
Perhaps the self-same song that found a path
  Through the sad heart of Ruth, when, sick for home,
    She stood in tears amid the alien corn;
      The same that oft-times hath
  Charm'd magic casements, opening on the foam
  Of perilous seas, in faery lands forlorn.

Forlorn! the very word is like a bell
  To toll me back from thee to my sole self!
Adieu! the fancy cannot cheat so well
  As she is famed to do, deceiving elf.
Adieu! adieu! thy plaintive anthem fades
  Past the near meadows, over the still stream,
    Up the hill-side; and now 'tis buried deep
      In the next valley-glades:
  Was it a vision, or a waking dream?
    Fled is that music:—do I wake or sleep?

ODE TO AUTUMN

Season of mists and mellow fruitfulness!
Close bosom-friend of the maturing sun;
Conspiring with him how to load and bless
With fruit the vines that round the thatch-eaves run;
To bend with apples the moss'd cottage-trees,
And fill all fruit with ripeness to the core;
To swell the gourd, and plump the hazel shells
With a sweet kernel; to set budding more

And still more, later flowers for the bees,
Until they think warm days will never cease;
For Summer has o'erbrimm'd their clammy cells.

Who hath not seen Thee oft amid thy store?
Sometimes whoever seeks abroad may find
Thee sitting careless on a granary floor,
Thy hair soft-lifted by the winnowing wind;
Or on a half-reap'd furrow sound asleep,
Drowsed with the fume of poppies, while thy hook
Spares the next swath and all its twinéd flowers;
And sometimes like a gleaner thou dost keep
Steady thy laden head across a brook;
Or by a cider-press, with patient look,
Thou watchest the last oozings, hours by hours.

Where are the songs of Spring? Aye, where are they?
Think not of them,—thou hast thy music too,
While barréd clouds bloom the soft-dying day
And touch the stubble-plains with rosy hue:
Then in a wailful choir the small gnats mourn
Among the river-sallows, borne aloft
Or sinking as the light wind lives or dies;
And full-grown lambs loud bleat from hilly bourn;
Hedge-crickets sing, and now with treble soft
The redbreast whistles from a garden-croft,
And gathering swallows twitter in the skies.

ON MELANCHOLY

No, no! go not to Lethe, neither twist
   Wolf's-bane, tight-rooted, for its poisonous wine;
Nor suffer thy pale forehead to be kiss'd
   By nightshade, ruby grape of Proserpine;
Make not your rosary of yew-berries,
   Nor let the beetle nor the death-moth be
     Your mournful Psyche, nor the downy owl
A partner in your sorrow's mysteries;
   For shade to shade will come too drowsily,
     And drown the wakeful anguish of the soul.

But when the melancholy fit shall fall
   Sudden from heaven like a weeping cloud,
That fosters the droop-headed flowers all,
   And hides the green hill in an April shroud;
Then glut thy sorrow on a morning rose,
   Or on the rainbow of the salt sand-wave,
     Or on the wealth of globéd peonies;
Or if thy mistress some rich anger shows,
   Emprison her soft hand, and let her rave,
     And feed deep, deep upon her peerless eyes.

She dwells with Beauty—Beauty that must die;
   And Joy, whose hand is ever at his lips
Bidding adieu; and aching Pleasure nigh,
   Turning to poison while the bee-mouth sips:
Ay, in the very temple of Delight
   Veil'd Melancholy has her sovran shrine,

>   Though seen of none save him whose strenuous tongue
>   Can burst Joy's grape against his palate fine:
>   His soul shall taste the sadness of her might,
>   And be among her cloudy trophies hung.

WALT WHITMAN (1819–1892)

ON THE BEACH AT NIGHT

On the beach at night,
Stands a child with her father,
Watching the east, the autumn sky.

Up through the darkness,
While ravening clouds, the burial clouds, in black masses spreading,
Lower sullen and fast athwart and down the sky,
Amid a transparent clear belt of ether yet left in the east,
Ascends large and calm the lord-star Jupiter,
And nigh at hand, only a very little above,
Swim the delicate sisters the Pleiades.

From the beach the child holding the hand of her father,
Those burial-clouds that lower victorious soon to devour all,
Watching, silently weeps.
Weep not, child,
Weep not, my darling,

With these kisses let me remove your tears,
The ravening clouds shall not long be victorious,
They shall not long possess the sky, they devour the stars only in apparition,
Jupiter shall emerge, be patient, watch again another night, the Pleiades shall emerge,
They are immortal, all those stars both silvery and golden shall shine out again,
The great stars and the little ones shall shine out again, they endure,
The vast immortal suns and the long-enduring pensive moons shall again shine.
Then dearest child mournest thou only for Jupiter?
Considerest thou alone the burial of the stars?

Something there is,
(With my lips soothing thee, adding I whisper,
I give thee the first suggestion, the problem and indirection),
Something there is more immortal even than the stars,
(Many the burials, many the days and nights, passing away),
Something that shall endure longer even than lustrous Jupiter,
Longer than sun or any revolving satellite,
Or the radiant sisters the Pleiades.

ALFRED, LORD TENNYSON (1809–1892)

ODE ON THE DEATH OF THE DUKE OF WELLINGTON

1

Bury the Great Duke
  With an empire's lamentation,
Let us bury the Great Duke
  To the noise of the mourning of a mighty nation,
Mourning when their leaders fall,
Warriors carry the warrior's pall,
And sorrow darkens hamlet and hall.

2

Where shall we lay the man whom we deplore?
Here, in streaming London's central roar,
Let the sound of those he wrought for,
And the feet of those he fought for,
Echo round his bones for evermore.

3

Lead out the pageant; sad and slow,
As fits an universal woe,
Let the long long procession go,
And let the sorrowing crowd about it grow,
And let the mournful martial music blow;
The last great Englishman is low.

Great Duke. Wellington died in 1852.

4

Mourn, for to us he seems the last,
Remembering all his greatness in the Past.
No more in soldier fashion will he greet
With lifted hand the gazer in the street.
O friends, our chief state-oracle is mute:
Mourn for the man of long-enduring blood,
The statesman-warrior, moderate, resolute,
Whole in himself, a common good.
Mourn for the man of amplest influence,
Yet clearest of ambitious crime,
Our greatest yet with least pretence,
Great in council and great in war,
Foremost captain of his time,
Rich in saving common-sense,
And, as the greatest only are,
In his simplicity sublime.
O good gray head which all men knew,
O voice from which their omens all men drew,
O iron nerve to true occasion true,
O fall'n at length that tower of strength
Which stood four-square to all the winds that blew!
Such was he whom we deplore.
The long self-sacrifice of life is o'er.
The great World-victor's victor will be seen no more.

5

All is over and done:
Render thanks to the Giver,
England, for thy son.
Let the bell be toll'd.
Render thanks to the Giver,

And render him to the mould.
Under the cross of gold
That shines over city and river,
There he shall rest for ever
Among the wise and the bold.
Let the bell be toll'd:
And a reverent people behold
The towering car, the sable steeds:
Bright let it be with its blazon'd deeds,
Dark in its funeral fold.
Let the bell be toll'd;
And a deeper knell in the heart be knoll'd;
And the sound of the sorrowing anthem roll'd
Thro' the dome of the golden cross;
And the volleying cannon thunder his loss;
He knew their voices of old.
For many a time in many a clime
His captain's ear has heard them boom
Bellowing victory, bellowing doom;
When he with those deep voices wrought,
Guarding realms and kings from shame;
With those deep voices our dead captain taught
The tyrant, and asserts his claim
In that dread sound to the great name,
Which he has worn so pure of blame,
In praise and in dispraise the same,
A man of well-attemper'd frame.
O civic muse, to such a name,
To such a name for ages long,
To such a name,
Preserve a broad approach of fame,
And ever-echoing avenues of song.

6

"Who is he that cometh, like an honour'd guest,
With banner and with music, with soldier and with priest,
With a nation weeping, and breaking on my rest?"
Mighty seaman, this is he
Was great by land as thou by sea.
Thine island loves thee well, thou famous man,
The greatest sailor since our world began.
Now, to the roll of muffled drums,
To thee the greatest soldier comes;
For this is he
Was great by land as thou by sea;
His foes were thine; he kept us free;
O give him welcome, this is he,
Worthy of our gorgeous rites,
And worthy to be laid by thee;
For this is England's greatest son,
He that gain'd a hundred fights,
Nor ever lost an English gun;
This is he that far away
Against the myriads of Assaye
Clash'd with his fiery few and won;
And underneath another sun,
Warring on a later day,
Round affrighted Lisbon drew
The treble works, the vast designs
Of his labour'd rampart-lines,
Where he greatly stood at bay,
Whence he issued forth anew,
And ever great and greater grew,
Beating from the wasted vines
Back to France her banded swarms,
Back to France with countless blows,

Till o'er the hills her eagles flew
Beyond the Pyrenean pines,
Follow'd up in valley and glen
With blare of bugle, clamour of men,
Roll of cannon and clash of arms,
And England pouring on her foes.
Such a war had such a close.
Again their ravening eagle rose
In anger, wheel'd on Europe-shadowing wings,
And barking for the thrones of kings;
Till one that sought but Duty's iron crown
On that loud sabbath shook the spoiler down;
A day of onsets of despair!
Dash'd on every rocky square
Their surging charges foam'd themselves away;
Last, the Prussian trumpet blew;
Thro' the long-tormented air
Heaven flash'd a sudden jubilant ray,
And down we swept and charged and overthrew.
So great a soldier taught us there,
What long-enduring hearts could do
In that world's-earthquake, Waterloo!
Mighty seaman, tender and true,
And pure as he from taint of craven guile,
O saviour of the silver-coasted isle,
O shaker of the Baltic and the Nile,
If aught of things that here befall
Touch a spirit among things divine,
If love of country move thee there at all,
Be glad, because his bones are laid by thine!
And thro' the centuries let a people's voice
In full acclaim,
A people's voice,
The proof and echo of all human fame,

A people's voice, when they rejoice
At civic revel and pomp and game,
Attest their great commander's claim
With honour, honour, honour, honour to him,
Eternal honour to his name.

7

A people's voice! we are a people yet.
Tho' all men else their nobler dreams forget
Confused by brainless mobs and lawless Powers;
Thank Him who isled us here, and roughly set
His Saxon in blown seas and storming showers,
We have a voice, with which to pay the debt
Of boundless love and reverence and regret
To those great men who fought, and kept it ours.
And keep it ours, O God, from brute control;
O Statesmen, guard us, guard the eye, the soul
Of Europe, keep our noble England whole,
And save the one true seed of freedom sown
Betwixt a people and their ancient throne,
That sober freedom out of which there springs
Our loyal passion for our temperate kings;
For, saving that, ye help to save mankind
Till public wrong be crumbled into dust,
And drill the raw world for the march of mind,
Till crowds at length be sane and crowns be just.
But wink no more in slothful overtrust.
Remember him who led your hosts;
He bad you guard the sacred coasts.
Your cannons moulder on the seaward wall;
His voice is silent in your council-hall
For ever; and whatever tempests lour
For ever silent; even if they broke

In thunder, silent; yet remember all
He spoke among you, and the Man who spoke;
Who never sold the truth to serve the hour,
Nor palter'd with Eternal God for power;
Who let the turbid streams of rumour flow
Thro' either babbling world of high and low;
Whose life was work, whose language rife
With rugged maxims hewn from life;
Who never spoke against a foe;
Whose eighty winters freeze with one rebuke
All great self-seekers trampling on the right:
Truth-teller was our England's Alfred named;
Truth-lover was our English Duke;
Whatever record leap to light
He never shall be shamed.

8

Lo, the leader in these glorious wars
Now to glorious burial slowly borne,
Follow'd by the brave of other lands,
He, on whom from both her open hands
Lavish Honour shower'd all her stars,
And affluent Fortune emptied all her horn.
Yea, let all good things await
Him who cares not to be great,
But as he saves or serves the state.
Not once or twice in our rough island-story,
The path of duty was the way to glory;
He that walks it, only thirsting
For the right, and learns to deaden
Love of self, before his journey closes,
He shall find the stubborn thistle bursting
Into glossy purples, which outredden

All voluptuous garden-roses.
Not once or twice in our fair island-story,
The path of duty was the way to glory:
He, that ever following her commands,
On with toil of heart and knees and hands,
Thro' the long gorge to the far light has won
His path upward, and prevail'd,
Shall find the toppling crags of Duty scaled
Are close upon the shining table-lands
To which our God Himself is moon and sun.
Such was he: his work is done:
But while the races of mankind endure,
Let his great example stand
Colossal, seen of every land,
And keep the soldier firm, the statesman pure:
Till in all lands and thro' all human story
The path of duty be the way to glory:
And let the land whose hearths he saved from shame
For many and many an age proclaim
At civic revel and pomp and game
And when the long-illumined cities flame,
Their ever-loyal iron leader's fame,
With honour, honour, honour, honour to him,
Eternal honour to his name.

9

Peace, his triumph will be sung
By some yet unmoulded tongue
Far on in summers that we shall not see:
Peace, it is a day of pain
For one about whose patriarchal knee
Late the little children clung:
O peace, it is a day of pain

ENGLISH ODES

For one, upon whose hand and heart and brain
Once the weight and fate of Europe hung.
Ours the pain, be his the gain!
More than is of man's degree
Must be with us, watching here
At this, our great solemnity.
Whom we see not we revere.
We revere, and we refrain
From talk of battles loud and vain,
And brawling memories all too free
For such a wise humility
As befits a solemn fane:
We revere, and while we hear
The tides of Music's golden sea
Setting toward eternity,
Uplifted high in heart and hope are we,
Until we doubt not that for one so true
There must be other nobler work to do
Than when he fought at Waterloo,
And Victor he must ever be.
For tho' the Giant Ages heave the hill
And break the shore, and evermore
Make and break, and work their will;
Tho' world on world in myriad myriads roll
Round us, each with different powers,
And other forms of life than ours,
What know we greater than the soul?
On God and Godlike men we build our trust.
Hush, the Dead March wails in the people's ears:
The dark crowd moves, and there are sobs and tears:
The black earth yawns: the mortal disappears;
Ashes to ashes, dust to dust;
He is gone who seem'd so great.—
Gone; but nothing can bereave him

Of the force he made his own
Being here, and we believe him
Something far advanced in State,
And that he wears a truer crown
Than any wreath that man can weave him.
Speak no more of his renown,
Lay your earthly fancies down,
And in the vast cathedral leave him.
God accept him, Christ receive him.

MATTHEW ARNOLD (1822–1888)

WESTMINSTER ABBEY

WHAT, for a term so scant
Our shining visitant
Cheer'd us, and now is pass'd into the night?
Could'st thou no better keep, O Abbey old,
The boon thy dedication-sign foretold,
The presence of that gracious inmate, light?—
A child of light appear'd;
Hither he came, late-born and long-desired,
And to men's hearts this ancient place endear'd;
What, is the happy glow so soon expired?

Rough was the winter eve;
Their craft the fishers leave,
And down over the Thames the darkness drew.

Shining visitant. The ode was written to commemorate the burial in Westminster Abbey of Arthur Penrhyn Stanley, Dean of Westminster.

One still lags last, and turns, and eyes the Pile
　Huge in the gloom, across in Thorney Isle,
King Sebert's work, the wondrous Minster new.
　　　　—'Tis Lambeth now, where then
They moor'd their boats among the bulrush stems;
　And that new Minster in the matted fen
The world-famed Abbey by the westering Thames.

　　　His mates are gone, and he
　　　For mist can scarcely see
A strange wayfarer coming to his side—
　Who bade him loose his boat, and fix his oar,
　And row him straightway to the further shore,
And wait while he did there a space abide.
　　　The fisher awed obeys,
That voice had note so clear of sweet command;
　Through pouring tide he pulls, and drizzling haze
And sets his freight ashore on Thorney strand.

　　　The Minster's outlined mass
　　　Rose dim from the morass,
And thitherward the stranger took his way.
　Lo, on a sudden all the Pile is bright!
　Nave, choir and transept glorified with light,
While tongues of fire on coign and carving play!
　　　And heavenly odours fair
Come streaming with the floods of glory in,
　And carols float along the happy air,
As if the reign of joy did now begin.

　　　Then all again is dark;
　　　And by the fisher's bark
The unknown passenger returning stands.

O Saxon fisher! thou hast had with thee
The fisher from the Lake of Galilee—
So saith he, blessing him with outspread hands;
    Then fades, but speaks the while:
At dawn thou to King Sebert shalt relate
  How his St. Peter's Church in Thorney Isle
Peter, his friend, with light did consecrate.

    Twelve hundred years and more
      Along the holy floor
Pageants have pass'd, and tombs of mighty kings
  Efface the humbler graves of Sebert's line,
  And, as years sped, the minster-aisles divine
Grew used to the approach of Glory's wings.
    Arts came, and arms, and law,
And majesty, and sacred form and fear;
  Only that primal guest the fisher saw,
Light, only light, was slow to reappear.

    The Saviour's happy light,
      Wherein at first was dight
His boon of life and immortality,
  In desert ice of subtleties was spent
  Or drown'd in mists of childish wonderment,
Fond fancies here, there false philosophy.
    And harsh the temper grew
Of men with mind thus darken'd and astray;
  And scarce the boon of life could struggle through,
For want of light which should the boon convey.

    Yet in this latter time
      The promise of the prime
Seem'd to come true at last, O Abbey old!
  It seem'd, a child of light did bring the dower

Foreshown thee in thy consecration-hour,
And in thy courts his shining freight unroll'd:
   Bright wits, and instincts sure,
And goodness warm, and truth without alloy,
  And temper sweet, and love of all things pure,
And joy in light, and power to spread the joy.

    And on that countenance bright
    Shone oft so high a light,
That to my mind there came how, long ago,
  Lay on the hearth, amid a fiery ring,
  The charm'd babe of the Eleusinian king—
His nurse, the Mighty Mother, will'd it so.
    Warm in her breast, by day,
He slumber'd, and ambrosia balm'd the child;
  But all night long amid the flames he lay,
Upon the hearth, and play'd with them, and smiled.

    But once, at midnight deep,
    His mother woke from sleep,
And saw her babe amidst the fire, and scream'd.
  A sigh the Goddess gave, and with a frown
  Pluck'd from the fire the child, and laid him down;
Then raised her face, and glory round her stream'd.
    The mourning-stole no more
Mantled her form, no more her head was bow'd;
  But raiment of celestial sheen she wore,
And beauty fill'd her, and she spake aloud:—

    "O ignorant race of man!
    Achieve your good who can,
If your own hands the good begun undo?

Charm'd babe. Demophoön, son of Celeus, King of Eleusis.

Had human cry not marr'd the work divine,
  Immortal had I made this boy of mine;
But now his head to death again is due
    And I have now no power
Unto this pious household to repay
  Their kindness shown me in my wandering hour."
—She spake, and from the portal pass'd away.

    The boy his nurse forgot,
    And bore a mortal lot.
Long since, his name is heard on earth no more.
  In some chance battle on Cithæron-side
  The nursling of the Mighty Mother died,
And went where all his fathers went before.
    —On thee too, in thy day
Of childhood, Arthur! did some check have power,
  That radiant though thou wert, thou couldst but stay,
Bringer of heavenly light, a human hour?

    Therefore our happy guest
    Knew care, and knew unrest,
And weakness warn'd him, and he fear'd decline.
  And in the grave he laid a cherish'd wife,
  And men ignoble harass'd him with strife,
And deadly airs his strength did undermine.
    Then from his Abbey fades
The sound beloved of his victorious breath;
  And light's fair nursling stupor first invades,
And next the crowning impotence of death.

    But hush! This mournful strain,
    Which would of death complain,

ENGLISH ODES

The oracle forbade, not ill inspired—
   That Pair, whose heads did plan, whose hands did forge
   The Temple in the pure Parnassian gorge,
Finish'd their work, and then a meed required.
      "Seven days," the God replied,
"Live happy, then expect your perfect meed!"
   Quiet in sleep, the seventh night, they died.
Death, death was judged the boon supreme indeed.

      And truly he who here
      Hath run his bright career,
And served men nobly, and acceptance found,
   And borne to light and right his witness high,
   What could he better wish than then to die,
And wait the issue, sleeping underground?
      Why should he pray to range
Down the long age of truth that ripens slow;
   And break his heart with all the baffling change,
And all the tedious tossing to and fro?

      For this and that way swings
      The flux of mortal things,
Though moving inly to one far-set goal—
   What had our Arthur gain'd, to stop and see,
   After light's term, a term of cecity,
A Church once large and then grown strait in soul?
      To live, and see arise,
Alternating with wisdom's too short reign,
   Folly revived, re-furbish'd sophistries,
And pullulating rites externe and vain?

      Ay me! 'Tis deaf, that ear
      Which joy'd my voice to hear;

That pair. The architects of the temple of Apollo at Delphi.

Yet would I not disturb thee from thy tomb,
  Thus sleeping in thine Abbey's friendly shade,
  And the rough waves of life for ever laid!
I would not break thy rest, nor change thy doom.
    Even as my father, thou—
Even as that loved, that well-recorded friend—
  Hast thy commission done; ye both may now
Wait for the leaven to work, the let to end.

    And thou, O Abbey grey!
    Predestined to the ray
By this dear guest over thy precinct shed—
  Fear not but that thy light once more shall burn,
  Once more thine immemorial gleam return,
Though sunk be now this bright, this gracious head
    Let but the light appear
And thy transfigured walls be touch'd with flame—
  Our Arthur will again be present here,
Again from lip to lip will pass his name.

CHARLES KINGSLEY (1819–1875)

ODE TO THE NORTH-EAST WIND

  Welcome, wild North-easter!
    Shame it is to see
  Odes to every zephyr;
    Ne'er a verse to thee.
  Welcome, black North-easter!
    O'er the German foam;

O'er the Danish moorlands,
  From thy frozen home.
Tired we are of summer,
  Tired of gaudy glare,
Showers soft and steaming,
  Hot and breathless air.
Tired of listless dreaming,
  Through the lazy day:
Jovial wind of winter,
  Turn us out to play!
Sweep the golden reed-beds:
  Crisp the lazy dyke;
Hunger into madness
  Every plunging pike.
Fill the lake with wild-fowl:
  Fill the marsh with snipe;
While on dreary moorlands
  Lonely curlew pipe.
Through the black fir-forest
  Thunder harsh and dry,
Shattering down the snow-flakes
  Off the curdled sky.
Hark! The brave North-easter!
  Breast-high lies the scent,
On by holt and headland,
  Over heath and bent.
Chime, ye dappled darlings,
  Through the sleet and snow.
Who can over-ride you?
  Let the horses go!
Chime, ye dappled darlings,
  Down the roaring blast;
You shall see a fox die
  Ere an hour be past.

Go! and rest to-morrow,
  Hunting in your dreams,
While our skates are ringing
  O'er the frozen streams.
Let the luscious South-wind
  Breathe in lovers' sighs,
While the lazy gallants
  Bask in ladies' eyes.
What does he but soften
  Heart alike and pen?
'Tis the hard grey weather
  Breeds hard English men.
What's the soft South-wester?
  'Tis the ladies' breeze,
Bringing home their true loves
  Out of all the seas:
But the black North-easter,
  Through the snowstorm hurled,
Drives our English hearts of oak
  Seaward round the world.
Come, as came our fathers,
  Heralded by thee,
Conquering from the eastward,
  Lords by land and sea.
Come; and strong within us
  Stir the Vikings' blood;
Bracing brain and sinew;
  Blow, thou wind of God!

ALGERNON CHARLES SWINBURNE
(1837-1909)

TO VICTOR HUGO

  In the fair days when God
  By man as godlike trod,
And each alike was Greek, alike was free,
  God's lightning spared, they said,
  Alone the happier head
Whose laurels screen'd it; fruitless grace for thee,
  To whom the high gods gave of right
Their thunders and their laurels and their light.

  Sunbeams and bays before
  Our master's servants wore,
For these Apollo left in all men's lands;
  But far from these ere now
  And watch'd with jealous brow
Lay the blind lightnings shut between God's hands,
  And only loosed on slaves and kings
The terror of the tempest of their wings.

  Born in those younger years
  That shone with storms of spears
And shook in the wind blown from a dead world's pyre,
  When by her back-blown hair
  Napoleon caught the fair
And fierce Republic with her feet of fire,
  And stay'd with iron words and hands
Her flight, and freedom in a thousand lands:

> Thou sawest the tides of things
> Close over heads of kings,
> And thine hand felt the thunder, and to thee
> Laurels and lightnings were
> As sunbeams and soft air
> Mix'd each in other, or as mist with sea
> Mix'd, or as memory with desire,
> Or the lute's pulses with the louder lyre.
>
> For thee man's spirit stood
> Disrobed of flesh and blood,
> And bare the heart of the most secret hours;
> And to thine hand more tame
> Than birds in winter came
> High hopes and unknown flying forms of powers,
> And from thy table fed, and sang
> Till with the tune men's ears took fire and rang.
>
> Even all men's eyes and ears
> With fiery sound and tears
> Wax'd hot, and cheeks caught flame and eyelid light,
> At those high notes of thine
> That stung the sense like wine,
> Or fell more soft than dew or snow by night,
> Or wailed as in some flooded cave
> Sobs the strong broken spirit of a wave.
>
> But we, our Master, we
> Whose hearts uplift to thee,
> Ache with the pulse of thy remember'd song,
> We ask not nor await
> From the clench'd hands of fate,
> As thou, remission of the world's old wrong;
> Respite we ask not, nor release;
> Freedom a man may have, he shall not peace.

> Though thy most fiery hope
> Storm heaven, to set wide ope
> The all-sought-for gate whence God or Chance debars
> All feet of men, all eyes—
> The old night resumes her skies,
> Her hollow hiding-place of clouds and stars
> Where nought save these is sure in sight;
> And, paven with death, our days are roof'd with night.
>
> One thing we can; to be
> Awhile, as men may, free;
> But not by hope or pleasure the most stern
> Goddess, most awful-eyed,
> Sits, but on either side
> Sit sorrow and the wrath of hearts that burn,
> Sad faith that cannot hope or fear,
> And memory grey with many a flowerless year.
>
> Not that in stranger's wise
> I lift not loving eyes
> To the fair foster-mother France, that gave
> Beyond the pale fleet foam
> Help to my sires and home,
> Whose great sweet breast could shelter those and save
> Whom from her nursing breast and hands
> Their land cast forth of old on gentler lands.
>
> Not without thoughts that ache
> For theirs and for thy sake,
> I, born of exiles, hail thy banish'd head;
> I whose young song took flight
> Towards the great heat and light
> On me a child from thy far splendour shed,
> From thine high place of soul and song,
> Which, fallen on eyes yet feeble, made them strong.

    Ah, not with lessening love
    For memories born hereof,
I look to that sweet mother-land, and see
    The old fields and fair full streams,
    And skies, but fled like dreams
The feet of freedom and the thought of thee;
    And all between the skies and graves
The mirth of mockers and the shame of slaves.

    She, kill'd with noisome air,
    Even she! and still so fair,
Who said, "Let there be freedom," and there was
    Freedom; and as a lance
    The fiery eyes of France
Touch'd the world's sleep, and as a sleep made pass
    Forth of men's heavier ears and eyes
Smitten with fire and thunder from new skies.

    Are they men's friends indeed
    Who watch them weep and bleed?
Because thou has loved us, shall the gods love thee?
    Thou, first of men and friend,
    Seest thou, even thou, the end?
Thou knowest what hath been, knowest thou what shall be?
    Evils may pass and hopes endure;
But fate is dim, and all the gods obscure.

    O nursed in airs apart,
    O poet highest of heart,
Hast thou seen time, who hast seen so many things?
    Are not the years more wise,
    More sad than keenest eyes,
The years with soundless feet and sounding wings?
    Passing we hear them not, but past
The clamour of them thrills us, and their blast.

      Thou art chief of us, and lord;
      Thy song is as a sword
Keen-edged and scented in the blade from flowers;
      Thou art lord and king; but we
      Lift younger eyes, and see
Less of high hope, less light on wandering hours;
      Hours that have borne men down so long,
Seen the right fail, and watch'd uplift the wrong.

      But thine imperial soul,
      As years and ruins roll
To the same end, and all things and all dreams
      With the same wreck and roar
      Drift on the dim same shore,
Still in the bitter foam and brackish streams
      Tracks the fresh water-spring to be
And sudden sweeter fountains in the sea.

      As once the high God bound
      With many a rivet round
Man's Saviour, and with iron nail'd him through,
      At the wild end of things,
      Where even his own bird's wings
Flagg'd, whence the sea shone like a drop of dew,
      From Caucasus beheld below
Past fathoms of unfathomable snow;

      So the strong God, the chance
      Central of circumstance,
Still shows him exile who will not be slave;
      All thy great fame and thee
      Girt by the dim strait sea
With multitudinous walls of wandering wave;
      Shows us our greatest from his throne,
Fate-stricken, and rejected of his own.

  Yea, he is strong, thou say'st,
  A mystery many-faced,
The wild beasts know him and the wild birds flee;
  The blind night sees him, death
  Shrinks beaten at his breath,
And his night hand is heavy on the sea;
  We know he hath made us, and is king;
We know not if he care for anything.

  Thus much, no more, we know;
  He bade what is be so,
Bade light be and bade night be, one by one;
  Bade hope and fear, bade ill
  And good redeem and kill,
Till all men be aweary of the sun
  And his world burn in its own flame
And bear no witness longer of his name.

  Yet though all this be thus,
  Be those men praised of us
Who have loved and wrought and sorrow'd and nor
    sinn'd
  For fame or fear or gold,
  Nor wax'd for winter cold,
Nor changed for changes of the worldly wind;
  Praised above men of men be these,
Till this one world and work we know shall cease.

  Yea, one thing more than this,
  We know that one thing is,
The splendour of a spirit without blame,
  That not the labouring years
  Blind-born, nor any fears,

Nor men nor any gods can tire or tame;
　　But purer power with fiery breath
Fills, and exalts above the gulfs of death.

　　　Praised above men be thou,
　　　Whose laurel-laden brow,
Made for the morning, droops not in the night;
　　　Praised and beloved, that none
　　　Of all thy great things done
Flies higher than thy most equal spirit's flight;
　　Praised, that nor doubt nor hope could bend
Earth's loftiest head, found upright to the end.

ARTHUR WILLIAM EDGAR O'SHAUGHNESSY (1844–1881)

ODE

We are the music-makers,
　　And we are the dreamers of dreams,
Wandering by lone sea-breakers,
　　And sitting by desolate streams;
World-losers and world-forsakers,
　　On whom the pale moon gleams:
Yet we are the movers and shakers
　　Of the world for ever, it seems.

With wonderful deathless ditties
We build up the world's great cities,
　　And out of a fabulous story
　　We fashion an empire's glory:

One man with a dream, at pleasure,
   Shall go forth and conquer a crown;
And three with a new song's measure
   Can trample a kingdom down.

We, in the ages lying
   In the buried past of the earth,
Built Nineveh with our sighing,
   And Babel itself in our mirth;
And o'erthrew them with prophesying
   To the Old of the New World's worth;
For each age is a dream that is dying,
   Or one that is coming to birth.

A breath of our inspiration
Is the life of each generation;
   A wondrous thing of our dreaming,
   Unearthly, impossible seeming—
The soldier, the king, and the peasant
   Are working together in one,
Till our dream shall become their present,
   And their work in the world be done.

They had no vision amazing
Of the goodly house they are raising,
   They had no divine foreshowing
   Of the land to which they are going:
But on one man's soul it hath broken,
   A light that doth not depart;
And his look, or a word he hath spoken,
   Wrought flame in another man's heart.

And therefore to-day is thrilling
With a past day's late fulfilling;

And the multitudes are enlisted
  In the faith that their fathers resisted,
And, scorning the dream of to-morrow,
  Are bringing to pass, as they may,
In the world, for its joy or its sorrow,
  The dream that was scorned yesterday.

But we, with our dreaming and singing,
  Ceaseless and sorrowless we!
The glory about us clinging
  Of the glorious future we see,
Our souls with high music ringing:
  O men! it must ever be
That we dwell, in our dreaming and singing,
  A little apart from ye.

For we are afar with the dawning
  And the suns that are not yet high,
And out of the infinite morning
  Intrepid you hear us cry—
How, spite of your human scorning,
  Once more God's future draws nigh,
And already goes forth the warning
  That ye of the past must die.

Great hail! we cry to the comers
  From the dazzling unknown shore;
Bring us hither your sun and your summers,
  And renew our world as of yore:
You shall teach us your song's new numbers
  And things that we dreamed not before;
Yea, in spite of a dreamer who slumbers,
  And a singer who sings no more.

COVENTRY PATMORE (1823-1896)

WINTER

I, SINGULARLY moved
To love the lovely that are not beloved,
Of all the Seasons, most
Love Winter, and to trace
The sense of the Trophonian pallor on her face.
It is not death, but plenitude of peace;
And the dim cloud that does the world unfold
Hath less the characters of dark and cold
Than warmth and light asleep;
And correspondent breathing seems to keep
With the infant harvest, breathing soft below
Its eider coverlet of snow.
Nor is in field or garden anything
But, duly look'd into, contains serene
The substance of things hoped for, in the Spring,
And evidence of Summer not yet seen.
On every chance-mild day
That visits the moist shaw,
The honeysuckle, 'sdaining to be crost
In urgence of sweet life by sleet or frost,
'Voids the time's law
With still increase
Of leaflet new, and little, wandering spray;

Trophonian. Trophonius is said to have built the temple of Apollo at Delphi. He had a temple at Lebadeia, and was worshipped as Jupiter Trophonius. In this temple was a cave, and those who descended into it were capable of speaking oracles afterwards, but the descent produced such saddening impressions that they remained the victims of melancholy for the rest of their lives.

Often, in sheltering brakes,
As one from rest disturb'd in the first hour,
Primrose or violet bewilder'd wakes,
And deems 'tis time to flower;
Though not a whisper of her voice he hear,
The buried bulb does know
The signals of the year,
And hails far Summer with his lifted spear;
The gorse-field dark, by sudden, gold caprice,
Turns, here and there, into a Jason's fleece;
Lilies that, soon in Autumn, slipp'd their gowns of green
And vanish'd into earth,
And came again, ere Autumn died, to birth,
Stand full-array'd amidst the wavering shower,
And perfect for the Summer, less the flower;
In nook of pale or crevice of crude bark,
Thou canst not miss,
If close thou spy, to mark
The ghostly chrysalis,
That, if thou touch it, stirs in its dream dark;
And the flush'd Robin, in the evenings hoar
Does of Love's Day, as if he saw it, sing.
But sweeter yet than dream or song of Summer or
      Spring
Are Winter's sometime smiles, that seem to well
From infancy ineffable;
Her wandering, languorous gaze,
So unfamiliar, so without amaze,
On the elemental, chill adversity,
The uncomprehended rudeness; and her sigh
And solemn, gathering tear,
And look of exile from some great repose, the sphere
Of ether, moved by ether only, or
By something still more tranquil.

MICHAEL FIELD

ODE TO DAWN

I breathe: the cloud below the night is breaking;
    The air uncloses:
Thou risest from thy couch. O Dawn, thy waking
    Is that of roses!
Thou child of Titan, how thy power prevails!
One sister hand touches the Moon that sails
Away, that sinks; one greets the sun, withheld
By the chill shadows thou art brave against.
What may not by thy buoyant cheer be quelled
Of dominance by which thou art increased?
    O Dawn so wondrous bright,
Thou canst by force of thy salubrity,
    From heaven's own height,
Compass thy will in heaven and earth and sea.

Thou art immortal, and thine eyes immortal
    Rest on the ocean,
The shore, the groves, the temple's open portal,
    On new-tuned motion
Of birds, and field and flock and starting team,
As if they were immortal—on the youth
That girt for toil or journey in thy gaze
Receives his immortality for truth,
And lifts to thee an almost stifled praise,

Michael Field. The pseudonym of Miss Katherine Bradley and Miss Edith Cooper. Miss Cooper died in 1913, and Miss Bradley in the following year.

			Thou bracest so his heart.
Yea, the whole burnished land, as if eterne
			In every part,
Doth toward thy face with equal glitter yearn.

And yearningly thou in thy course dost linger,
			With gracious boldness,
O'er Cephalus laid sleeping, and thy finger,
			A rose-bud coldness,
Startles and pricks him till the boy awakes,
Who, smiled at from thine honest eyes, forgets
His first sigh for his Procris: to thy car
Thou dost constrain him captive, and with speed,
Beyond the lark-glint with the morning-star,
Discouraging the heaven with thy deed,
			Thou and thy coursers glow,
On towards Olympus where thou facest all
			The wise gods know,
Nor can their congregated eyes appal.

Thy chastity is in thy will, thy beauty
			Is eager flushing.
On him thou lov'st thou layest as love's duty,
			(All terror hushing)
From earth steeply to travel at thy side,
Till by adventure he be deified.
Not Cephalus alone, Orion too,
And young Tithonus thou hast borne above.
No matter should the mortal prove untrue,
And pine in stupor for an earthly love,
			Or hurled down from the sky
Be sunk in waves, or 'mid the heavenly born
			See Age draw nigh
To snow upon a single head forlorn.

It is thy impulse of inviolate willing
        Stirs glade and mountain.
The nests in arbour, birds beside the rilling
        Of forest fountain,
The wood-flowers and the stream-flowers and all things
Would drive aloft with thee. Ah, thou hast wings!
Most lovable, forget not what thou art:
Thou drawest us to thee, to heaven remain.
Intrepid dreamers, to the clouds we start,
And smile with thee along, with thee attain
        The gods, the placid Throne;
Then 'mid the hollow vapours of the way
        We wake alone,
O rose-hung queen of steeds—and lo, 'tis day.

Spare thou the flowers! Let not their discs be flattered
        With lofty dreaming
Of Hera's bosom and her pavement scattered
        With their first beaming:
Let not the bird tune for Apollo's thanks
Where, voicing heaven, he crowds the happier banks.
Vain prayer! Most merciless of visions, shown
Too often to thy victims, yet so fresh
That never as a custom may we own
Thy presence, but are dazzled in thy mesh
        And suffer thy strong goad;
Deluded, brilliant with each new daybreak,
        Thy chiming road,
Even to the end, we and our world must take.

ROBERT BRIDGES

ODE ON THE TERCENTENARY COMMEMORATION OF SHAKESPEARE, 1916

KIND dove-wing'd Peace, for whose green olive-crown
The noblest kings would give their diadems,
  Mother, who hast ruled our home so long,
    How suddenly art thou fled!
Leaving our cities astir with war;
And yet on the fair fields deserted
Lingerest, wherever the gaudy seasons
  Deck with excessive splendour
  The sorrow-stricken year,
Where cornlands bask and high elms rustle gently,
And still the unweeting birds sing on by brae and bourn.

The trumpet blareth and calleth the true to be stern:
Be then thy soft reposeful music dumb;
  Yet shall thy lovers awhile give ear
    —An' tho' full-arm'd they come—
To the praise of England's gentlest son;
Whom, when she bore the Muses lov'd
Above the best of eldest honour
  —Yea, save one without peer—
  And by great Homer set,
Not to impugn his undisputed throne,
The myriad-hearted by the mighty-hearted one.

  For God of His gifts pour'd on him a full measure,
  And gave him to know Nature and the ways of men:
    And he dower'd with inexhaustible treasure

A world conquering speech,
　　Which surg'd as a river high-descended
　　That, gathering tributaries of many lands,
　　Rolls through the plain a bounteous flood,
　　　　Picturing towers and temples
　　　　And ruin of bygone times,
　　And floateth the ships deep-laden with merchandise
Out to the windy seas to traffic in foreign climes.

　　Thee, SHAKESPEARE, to-day we honour; and evermore
　　Since England bore thee, the master of human song,
　　　　Thy folk are we, children of thee,
　　　　　Who, knitting in one her realm
　　　　And strengthening with pride her sea-borne clans,
　　　　Scorn'st in the grave the bruize of death.
　　　　All thy later-laurel'd choir
　　　　　Laud thee in thy world-shrine:
　　　　　London's laughter is thine;
　　One with thee is our temper in melancholy or might,
And in thy book Great Britain's rule readeth her right.

　　Her chains are chains of Freedom, and her bright arms
　　Honour, Justice and Truth and Love to man.
　　　　Though first from a pirate ancestry
　　　　　She took her home on the wave,
　　　　Her gentler spirit arose disdainful,
　　　　And, smiting the fetters of slavery,
　　　　Made the high seaways safe and free,
　　　　　In wisdom bidding aloud
　　　　　To world-wide brotherhood,
　　Till her flag was hail'd as the ensign of Liberty,
And the boom of her guns went round the earth in
　　salvoes of peace.

And thou, when Nature bow'd her mastering hand
To borrow an ecstacy of man's art from thee,
  Thou, her poet, secure as she
    Of the shows of eternity,
  Didst never fear thy work should fall
  To fashion's craze nor pedant's folly
  Nor devastator, whose arrogant arms
    Murder and maim mankind;
    Who, when in scorn of grace
He hath batter'd and burn'd some loveliest dearest
    shrine.
Laugheth in ire and boasteth aloud his brazen god.

   .   .   .   .   .   .

I saw the Angel of Earth from strife aloof
Mounting the heavenly stair with Time on high,
  Growing ever younger in the brightening air
    Of the everlasting dawn:
  It was not terror in his eyes nor wonder,
  That glance of the intimate exaltation
  Which lieth as Power under all Being,
    And broodeth in Thought above—
    As a bird wingeth over the ocean,
Whether indolently the heavy water sleepeth
Or is dash'd in a million waves, chafing or lightly laughing.

  I hear his voice in the music of lamentation,
  In echoing chant and cadenced litany,
    In country song and pastoral piping
      And silvery dances of mirth:
    And oft, as the eyes of a lion in the brake,
    His presence hath startled me . . .
    In austere shapes of beauty lurking,

Beautiful for Beauty's sake;
   As a lonely blade of life
 Ariseth to flower, whenever the unseen Will
Stirreth with kindling aim the dark fecundity of Being.

 Man knoweth but as in a dream of his own desire
   The thing that is good for man, and he dreameth well:
     But the lot of the gentle heart is hard
       That is cast in an epoch of life
     When evil is knotted and demons fight,
     Who know not, they, that the lowest lot
     Is treachery, hate and trust in sin
       And perseverance in ill,
       Doom'd to oblivious Hell,
 To pass with the shames unspoken of men away,
Wash'd out with tombs by the grey unpitying tears of
   Heaven.

 But ye, dear Youth, who lightly in the day of fury
   Put on England's glory as a common coat,
     And in your stature of masking grace
       Stood forth warriors complete,
     No praise o'ershadoweth yours to-day,
     Walking out of the home of love
     To match the deeds of all the dead.—
       Alas! alas! fair Peace,
       These were thy blossoming roses.
   Look on thy shame, fair Peace, thy tearful shame!
 Turn to thine isle, fair Peace; return thou and guard it
     well!

JOHN MASEFIELD

THE KINGS GO BY WITH JEWELLED CROWNS

The Kings go by with jewelled crowns;
Their horses gleam, their banners shake, their spears are
    many.
The sack of many-peopled towns
Is all their dream;
The way they take
Leaves but a ruin in the brake,
And, in the furrow that the ploughmen make,
A stampless penny: a tale, a dream.

The merchants reckon up their gold;
Their letters come, their ships arrive, their freights are
    glories;
The profits of their treasures sold
They tell and sum;
Their foemen drive
The servants starved to half-alive,
Whose labours do but make the earth a hive
Of stinking stories: a tale, a dream.

The priests are singing in their stalls;
Their singing lifts, their incense burns, their praying
    clamours;
Yet God is as the sparrow falls;
The ivy drifts,
The votive urns
Are all left void when Fortune turns;
The god is but a marble for the kerns
To break with hammers: a tale, a dream.

O Beauty, let me know again
The green earth cold, the April rain, the quiet waters,
    figuring sky,
The one star risen.

So shall I pass into the feast
Not touched by king, merchant, or priest;
Know the red spirit of the beast,
Be the green grain;
Escape from prison.

LASCELLES ABERCROMBIE

CEREMONIAL ODE INTENDED FOR A UNIVERSITY

WHEN from Eternity were separate
    The curdled element
And gathered forces, and the world began,—
The Spirit that was shut and darkly blent
Within this being, did the whole distress
With a blind hanker after spaciousness.
    Into its wrestle, strictly tied up in Fate
And closely natured, came like an open'd grate
    At last the Mind of Man,
Letting the sky in, and a faculty
To light the cell with lost Eternity.

So commerce with the Infinite was regain'd:
    For upward grew Man's ken
And trode with founded footsteps the grievous fen
Where other life festering and prone remained.

With knowledge painfully quarried and hewn fair,
Platforms of lore, and many a hanging stair
Of strong imagination Man has raised
His wisdom like the watch-towers of a town;
   That he, though fasten'd down
In law, be with its cruelty not amazed,
But be of outer vastness greatly aware.

This, then, is yours: to build exultingly
   High, and yet more high,
The knowledgeable towers above base wars
And sinful surges reaching up to lay
Dishonouring hands upon your work, and drag
From their uprightness your desires to lag
Among low places with a common gait.
That so Man's mind, not conquer'd by his clay,
   May sit above his fate,
Inhabiting the purpose of the stars,
And trade with his Eternity.

COMMENTARY

THE DEVELOPMENT OF THE ODE

THE ode, like so many other forms of poetry, originated in Greece, and was, in its earliest form, a poem to be sung to the accompaniment of some musical instrument. It was thus a branch of lyrical poetry: the word lyrical again suggesting the use of a musical accompaniment. Among the Greeks this lyrical poetry, or, to give it the more usual Greek name, *melic* poetry, was always poetry to be sung; and as such it was clearly differentiated from poetry like epic poetry which was intended for recitation. In this melic poetry, the music was always an essential and integral portion of the work.

In the hands of the Greek poets melic poetry developed along two main lines, of which one was the form we now perhaps associate more particularly with the word lyric: the song which gives utterance to a poet's own feelings and emotions, and is intended to be sung by one singer only. Among the Æolians this simpler form resulted in the seventh century B.C. in the production of many beautiful lyrics, whose singers include the world-famed Alcæus, Sappho and Anacreon.

But alongside this lighter and more personal odic form, there developed also, among the Dorian people, a much more elaborate form, which reflected the severity, the discipline, and the steadfastness characteristic of Dorian life. It treated in stately fashion of some event other than a poet's personal feelings or emotions and developed into a great choric song, raised in praise of

THE DEVELOPMENT OF THE ODE

victory at the Olympic or other famous games, or sung in celebration of a marriage, or as a dirge for someone lost, or as a song to celebrate the foundation of a city or a temple or the festival of the worship of some national or local deity.

Such great Choral Odes required a much more elaborate treatment than the simpler personal Æolian form. A company of singers was necessary for their performance, together with musicians with pipe and flute and lyre; and these participants were also an orchestra of trained dancers, who moved in rhythmic fashion as they sang. All three parts, song, music and dance, were closely linked and interwoven, and all three were essential, though the song remained always the most important part, and music and dance were subordinated in all cases to the poet's words.

Choral song became an important element in the great Athenian dramas of Æschylus, Sophocles, and Euripides; as a separate lyrical form it was elaborated by a succession of poets, and received its final treatment at the hands of the famous poets Simonides (556–468 B.C.) and Pindar (522–443 B.C.). Under the inspiration of these poets these great Choral Odes assumed a form in which the stanzas were arranged in groups of three; the first stanza being termed the *Strophe*; the second, the *Antistrophe*; the third, the *Epode*. There is no single definite form of strophic or other stanza; indeed the stanzaic variations are many in number, and no two remaining Pindaric Odes have the same metrical structure. But in any given ode all the strophic stanzas must be of the same form, and all the antistrophic stanzas must correspond completely with the strophic; the epodic stanzas may and will differ from the strophic, but must agree with one another throughout the one ode. This variation seems to have originated in the movements of the orchestra. The strophe was sung as the dancers moved forward to the right; the antistrophe commenced when they turned for their second movement to the left; the epode occupied a period of rest which followed these movements: and so on through the course of the ode.

It was this elaborated form that Pindar used in his world-famed odes, and he added to the difficulties caused by this form other difficulties due to the great rapidity and wilful obscurity of his thought, and the purposely archaic character of his language. A daring use of metaphor and the clever utilisation of Hellenic myth and legend were also characteristics of his style.

It is impossible for us to understand the full effect of the Pindaric Ode upon the poet's hearers, for the music associated with the odes has been lost; and either because of this loss, or from inability to comprehend the construction of the odes, or from some other cause, the Latin poets, who were always ready to adopt Greek forms when possible, made no attempt to imitate Pindar's work. They preferred the simpler and more regular lyrical forms that Anacreon and Sappho and their followers had used, and copied them effectively; so much so, in fact, that this type of ode is now most frequently spoken of in its association with Latin poets like Horace and Catullus.

With the decay of Latin literature the ode disappeared, to be revived, as was natural, in the days of the Renaissance; at first in France, where its life was very short, and next in England, where the poets used the simpler forms with great success. Our selection includes one of the first of these attempts, the beautiful *Prothalamion* of Edmund Spenser, a series of stanzas with an intricate rhyming scheme and delicate refrain, the

THE DEVELOPMENT OF THE ODE 171

whole forming one of the most beautiful of all English odes. In the hands of Ben Jonson and his disciples the ode became a more or less regular lyric, made up of a series of regular stanzas, with or without a refrain. We should expect so splendid a classical scholar as Milton, and one so interested as he was in experiments in prosody, to attempt this form, and we are not disappointed. He wrote several poems of this kind; one of them, *The Hymn on the Morning of Christ's Nativity*, written by him at the age of twenty-one, is one of our finest odes.

All these efforts, however, had been in the simpler form; the more elaborate Pindaric Ode had not been attempted; the basis on which these intricate choral songs had been built was not understood by their readers.

Those who attempted odes in the Pindaric manner believed that they were altogether formless, and explained this formlessness as the result of the "divine frenzy" which so possessed the poet at the moment of inspiration and exaltation as to cause him to neglect form in the rapidity of his utterance. In 1645, however, the poet Cowley, exiled in France as a result of his efforts for the Stuart cause, began to read Pindar's works; drawn to them in the first instance, as he tells us, by the fact that they were the only book he could obtain. In reading them he missed entirely the careful and elaborate scheme on which they were built up, and thought their apparent irregularity was part of the poet's purpose, and resulted from the emotion which possessed him as he wrote. Cowley began to write what he considered to be Imitations of these Odes; and his preface to his Pindaric Odes makes his point of view quite clear. He is in great doubt whether his odes will be understood by those who are well enough acquainted with the common roads and ordinary tracks of Poesie; and this because "the figures are unusual and bold, even to Temeritie, and such as I durst not have to do withal in any other kind of poetry: the numbers are various and irregular, and sometimes (especially some of the long ones) seem harsh and uncouth, if the just measures and cadencies be not obscured in the pronunciation. So that almost all their sweetness and numerosity (which is to be found, if I mistake not, in the roughest, if rightly repeated) lies in a manner wholly at the mercy of the reader."

In the last stanza of his ode entitled *The Resurrection* he enters into a description of the "Pindarique Pegasus" as he conceives him:

> 'Tis an unruly, and a hard-mouth'd horse,
>   Fierce and unbroken yet,
> Impatient of the spur or bit,
> Now praunces stately, and anon flies o'er the place,
> Disdains the servile law of any settled pace,
> Conscious and proud of his own natural force,
>   'Twill no unskilful touch endure,
> But flings writer and reader too that sits not sure.

And his note to this ode is that it is a "truly Pindarical Ode."

Unfortunately these formless, harsh and irregular Odes of Cowley became very popular, and many elaborate odes of a similar kind were composed by writers of but little poetic ability, while the better poets continued to write in the Horatian form, Marvell's *Horatian Ode* being one of the very best examples of this kind in the language; though Dryden also produced odes in the irregular form with great success. The first Englishman to realise that these irregular odes were certainly not Pindaric was Congreve. He studied Pindar's works, and discovered what Pindar was aiming at in his construction: and he explained the basis of the Pindaric

THE DEVELOPMENT OF THE ODE

form in a preface to an ode addressed to Queen Anne in honour of Marlborough's famous victories (1706). Unfortunately Congreve's practice was by no means equal to his scholarly theory, and his poetic work had but little value or influence.

About forty years later Gilbert West continued Congreve's work and explained Pindar's constructions and methods once more, with translations from Pindar's Odes as examples. It was West's efforts that inspired Gray to attempt this form, and so gave us *The Bard* and *The Progress of Poesy*, two excellent examples of the Pindaric Ode. Collins, too, attempted this form, though he preferred the Horatian type. This Horatian form, indeed, still remained the favourite and helped to bring about what we may perhaps call the English form; an ode developed in a series of more or less regular stanzas, as Spenser's *Prothalamion* had been. Keats, especially, who speaks of

> the grandeur of the ode,
> Growing like Atlas, stronger from its load,

utilised the stanzaic form, and in his hands the English ode reached its most splendid heights. Wordsworth used both regular and irregular forms, Coleridge preferred the irregular, Shelley and Byron wrote stanzaic odes, but with much irregularity.

In the nineteenth century there developed a very decided tendency in favour of a totally irregular form (rhymeless Pindarics, Mr. Saintsbury calls these odes); they frequently dispense with rhyme altogether, and in their varied length of line and stanza approximate in many cases to *vers libre*. Patmore, Tennyson and other modern writers have written in this form with great success; many other modern poets are now using the form also.

We have, therefore, in English poetry at least three different classes or types of ode; the regular ode which follows the Æolian or Horatian tradition and is written in a succession of regular stanzas; the ode based upon the Pindaric tradition with its division into strophe, antistrophe, and epode; and the irregular ode which obeys neither of these forms, but proceeds upon its own path, with or without stanza, and with or without rhyme. Examples of all three classes are to be found in this selection of English odes; and the students' reading in English literature will bring them face to face continually with fresh examples. Unfortunately, the ode became the usual and recognised form for Poets Laureate called upon to sing of some important national or royal event, even though the inspiration might be lacking at the moment: and as a result of these forced productions, there are probably more feeble poems of this particular type than of any other type of English verse. But where mastery of the form is conjoined with poetic inspiration and enthusiasm, the result is a poem of the highest value, as the examples given in this selection sufficiently prove.

QUESTIONS AND EXERCISES

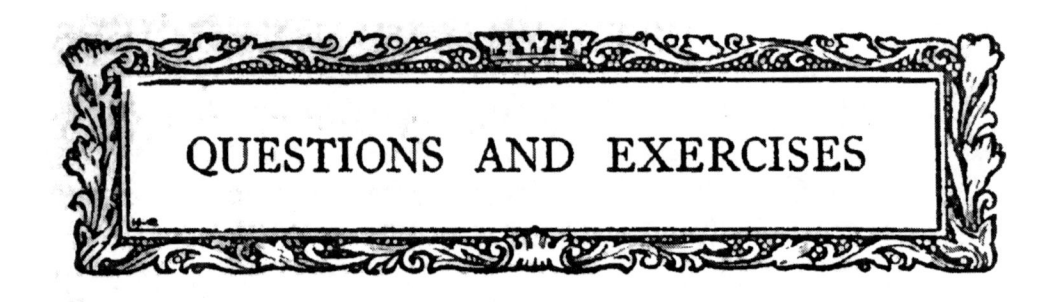

PROTHALAMION

1. Write down the rhyme-scheme of the stanza here employed. Does the refrain help the poem?

2. What information about the poet's own life may we gather from this poem? Show that the poet is "a child of the Renaissance."

3. It has been suggested that this ode gives the "sensation of music imprisoned." Consider this, and also Coleridge's feeling of "the swan-like movement of the lines."

TO HIMSELF

1. Write out Jonson's estimate of the play-going public of 1629, as he gives it in this ode. Would it at all fit the present age?

2. Jonson was undoubtedly one of the finest critics of his age. It would be interesting, therefore, to read his *New Inn* and compare it with his better-known dramatic work; and then see whether this vigorous denunciation of his audience is altogether justified.

TO MASTER ANTHONY STAFFORD

1. Does the poem suggest that Randolph knew more of country life or of town life?

2. Analyse the construction of the stanza of this poem; and compare with that of Jonson's *To Himself*.

QUESTIONS AND EXERCISES

ODE ON THE MORNING OF CHRIST'S NATIVITY

1. Do you find in this ode (written by Milton at the age of twenty-one) any suggestion of Puritan spirit?

2. To what extent does the ode seem to you the work of a young man who is living during the Renaissance period, and has spent some years as a student? Examine especially the sources from which Milton draws his material.

3. Consider the following appreciations:

Nowhere, even in Milton, does the mastery of harmonies appear better than in the exquisite rhythmical arrangement of the piece, in the almost unearthly beauty of the exordium, and in the famous stanzas beginning "The oracles are dumb."—SAINTSBURY.

The learning displayed shows that Milton was the poet of the study rather than of the market-place or field.—SARGEAUNT.

AT A SOLEMN MUSIC

1. Why are Voice and Verse sirens? and why sphere-born?

2. Are there any signs of the Milton of *Paradise Lost* in these early efforts of Milton? Are there any evidences of *youth* in them?

3. "Human language, at all events in English, has never surpassed in ecstasy of spiritual elevation or in pure passion of melody this little canzonet." Consider this.

BRUTUS

1. To what extent do you think Cowley was reading into the lives of Brutus, Cæsar, etc., the history of his own times, the death of Charles, the successful usurpation (as it seemed to him) of Cromwell, etc.?

2. On page 172 of this book is a quotation from Abraham Cowley giving his conception of what a Pindaric Ode should be. Having read that quotation, it will be interesting to re-read the *Brutus* and consider how nearly Cowley attains his ideal.

QUESTIONS AND EXERCISES

HORATIAN ODE UPON CROMWELL'S RETURN FROM IRELAND

1. How true do you consider Marvell's estimates of Cromwell and Charles?

2. Are you able to discover any resemblances to the Miltonic style in this ode?

TO BEN JONSON

1. Like Randolph, Herrick was a disciple of Ben Jonson, and acknowledges this gracefully in this short ode. See Beaumont's poem, *The Mermaid Tavern*, and read Herrick's *Prayer to Ben Jonson*.

2. Consider the construction of this ode.

SONG FOR SAINT CECILIA'S DAY

1. The structure of both these irregular odes which follow the tradition of Cowley is worthy of examination.

2. To what extent has Dryden succeeded in making his rhythms suggest the tones of the various instruments he mentions, and the effect of their music?

ALEXANDER'S FEAST, OR, THE POWER OF MUSIC

1. Consider (*a*) the poet's use of the refrain; (*b*) his success in suggesting by his poetry the different emotions aroused by the music of Timotheus.

2. Consider the following criticisms by Dr. Johnson:

The conclusion (of the first ode) is striking, but it includes an image so awful in itself, that it can owe little to poetry; and I could wish the antithesis of *music untuning* had found some other place.

The conclusion (of the second ode) is vicious; the music of Timotheus which raised a mortal to the skies had only a metaphorical power; that of Cecilia, which drew an angel down, had a real effect; the crown, therefore, could not reasonably be divided.

A PINDARIQUE ODE

1. Compare the construction of this ode with Cowley's *Brutus*, with Gray's *Progress of Poesy* or *The Bard*, and with the description of the Pindaric Ode on pages 169, 170.

2. Consider Congreve's use (or abuse) of classical and other allusion in this ode.

3. Compare Congreve's treatment in this ode with Tennyson's in his *Ode on the Death of the Duke of Wellington*.

TO FEAR

Which is the *thrice hallowed eve* to which Collins refers?

TO EVENING

Compare with Marvell's Horatian Ode.

THE PASSIONS

1. It is interesting to compare Collins' rendering of the effects of the Passions with Dryden's rendering in his odes. Note also the beauty of Collins' Invocations.

2. Consider the effect of the absence of rhyme in the *Ode to Evening*.

3. Compare these estimates of Collins:

His diction was often harsh, unskilfully laboured, and injudiciously selected. He affected the obsolete when it was not worthy of revival, and put words out of the common order.... His lines commonly are of slow motion, clogged and impeded with clusters of consonants.—JOHNSON.

His odes are bright, solemn, and serene.—WORDSWORTH.

The *Ode to Evening* has a fine tone of tranquil musing, even the objects of the surrounding landscape, by which the picture is completed are seen only in their reflections in the poet's mind.—MOY THOMAS.

QUESTIONS AND EXERCISES

ODE ON A DISTANT PROSPECT OF ETON COLLEGE

1. Consider the poet's use of (*a*) inversion; (*b*) personification in this poem.
2. Write out the rhyme-scheme of the stanza employed.

THE PROGRESS OF POESY

1. *III.* 3. The reference is to Dryden's odes. Do these odes of Gray owe anything to Dryden?
2. Consider Gray's estimate of Shakespeare, Milton and Dryden in this poem.
3. To what extent is this poem a true Pindaric ode? (see page 169.)
4. One critic calls this ode "the harbinger of the romantic movement"; another, "the last splendid utterance of a dying classicism." Is it possible to reconcile these criticisms?

THE BARD

1. Who is the *sable warrior* here referred to?
2. *II.* 2. Consider the last lines of this stanza as a description of the reign of Richard II., and the next stanza (*II.* 3) as a description of the Wars of the Roses. Who are the famous father; the meek usurper; the bristled boar; whose the infant-gore?
3. Compare these splendid Pindaric odes with Congreve's attempt.
4. Consider Gray's use of history in this ode, and especially his use of the device of *historical anticipation.*

ODE ON THE PLEASURE ARISING FROM VICISSITUDE

1. Compare the stanza here employed with that used in the *Ode on a Distant Prospect of Eton College,* and contrast with the form and stanza of his Pindaric odes.

ODE TO WINTER

1. Compare with Keats's *Ode to Autumn*.
2. Work out the rhyme scheme of the ode.

BATTLE OF THE BALTIC

1. Campbell was very much interested in ballad poetry. Is there evidence of this in these odes?
2. Mr. Herford says that this poet's "sublimity hovers near the verge of the melodramatic." Consider this.
3. Compare the *Battle of the Baltic* with other patriotic odes in this volume.

ODE TO DUTY

1. Wordsworth wrote: "Every great poet is a teacher. I wish either to be considered as a teacher, or as nothing." Do you think that the poet achieves his desire in these odes?
2. Mr. Hardy thought this ode "somewhat astringent." Consider this estimate.

ODE ON INTIMATIONS OF IMMORTALITY FROM RECOLLECTIONS OF EARLY CHILDHOOD

1. Students should read the poet's *Lines composed a Few Miles above Tintern Abbey*, 1798, and *The Prelude*, Books I. and II., and compare his descriptions of his childhood in these poems with the ideas on the meaning and importance of childhood given in this ode.
2. This ode is generally considered to be the finest ode in the English language. Students should examine its metrical structure.
3. Does Wordsworth find compensation for the loss of "the visionary gleam," and "the glory and the dream" which belong to youth in "the faith that looks through death," and "in years that bring the philosophic mind"?

DEJECTION: AN ODE

1. This ode is a poem of *intensely personal expression*, and also "a storehouse of splendid poetry, set to wild and changeful music." "It is in itself the closest self-revelation almost ever written. Only one other poem of his is more sorrowful, more like despair, more self-revealing—the poem addressed in 1807 to Wordsworth after reading *The Prelude*." (Stopford Brooke.) Examine the ode from these points of view.

2. "The ode *Dejection* is an infinitely pathetic qualification of the Wordsworthian faith in the power of Nature to impress and restore." Compare Coleridge's thoughts on Nature with those of Wordsworth in the *Ode on Intimations of Immortality*.

TO WORDSWORTH

1. Compare this Ode to Wordsworth with that poet's own odes, and especially with *Laodamia* (Landor mentions Laodameia's love forlorn in this ode) and the *Ode to Lycoris*.

2. It is interesting to compare what Landor here says about the great English poets with what Gray writes about them in his *Progress of Poesy*. Can you account for Landor's distaste for Spenser?

ODE ON VENICE

1. Byron's descriptions of Venice are amongst the finest passages that he wrote. Compare with this ode the description of Venice with which Canto iv. of *Childe Harold* commences. In Stanza xviii. he writes:

> I loved her from my boyhood,—she to me
> Was as a fairy city of the heart,
> Rising like water-columns from the sea,
> Of joy the sojourn, and of wealth the mart;
> And Otway, Radcliffe, Schiller, Shakespeare's art,
> Had stamped her image in me, and even so,
> Although I found her thus, we did not part,
> Perchance even dearer in her day of woe,
> Than when she was a boast, a marvel, and a show.

2. Which do you prefer, the ode, or the description in *Childe Harold*? Why?

TO LIBERTY

1. In reading this ode it is well to remember its date of composition, viz. 1820. What was the state of Europe at this time?

2. Analyse the structure of the stanza employed and compare with the stanzas used by Keats.

3. Trace the progress of Liberty from age to age as described by the poet in this ode; and comment upon Shelley's conception of *liberty*.

ODE TO THE WEST WIND

1. Shelley tells us that this poem "was conceived and chiefly written in a wood that skirts the Arno, near Florence, and on a day when that tempestuous wind, whose temperature is at once mild and animating, was collecting the vapours which pour down the autumnal rains."

2. Consider the treatment of Nature in this ode. Mr. Stopford Brooke writes:

He chooses such things in nature as are in tune with his soul, and then fuses himself and nature both together into one imagination.

This is written of Coleridge; is it also true of Shelley?

3. The prosody of the poem merits much consideration. Examine it in the light of the following analysis by Mr. Saintsbury:

The ode has the peculiarity of being in batches of five quatorzains; each divided into four triplets and a couplet, and almost invariably run together. It is really a kind of sonnet sequence, though the triplets, separately regarded, are *terza-rima*.

TO A SKYLARK

1. "Our sweetest songs are those that tell of saddest thought." Is this true of this poem, and of the *Ode to the West Wind*?

QUESTIONS AND EXERCISES

2. Compare the thoughts and emotions aroused in Shelley by the skylark with those aroused in Keats by the nightingale.

ON A GRECIAN URN

1. Read the sonnet, "On first looking into Chapman's Homer."

2. Consider the structure of the stanza in this and the other odes in this selection.

3. Mr. Herford says:

> In Keats the worship of beauty became supreme.

Consider this; and also the following:

The second and third stanzas express with perfect poetic felicity and insight the vital differences between life, which pays for its unique prerogative of reality by satiety and decay; and art, which in forfeiting reality gains in exchange permanence of beauty and the power to charm by imagined experiences even richer than the real.—COLVIN.

ODE TO A NIGHTINGALE

1. Compare Keats's feeling for Nature as here expressed, with Wordsworth's or Shelley's.

2. Much time could be spent to great advantage in examining Keats's use of words in these odes: full-throated ease; deep-delvéd earth; sun-burnt mirth; beaded bubbles winking at the brim; leaden-eyed despairs; embalméd darkness; darkling; alien corn; forlorn.

ODE TO AUTUMN

1. This vivid description of an English autumn breathes a spirit of happy contentment not always present in Keats's work.

2. Consider the fitness of the thought and music to the season they celebrate; and the beauty of the personification of autumn in the second stanza.

3. Read Shelley's *Ode to the West Wind* again.

QUESTIONS AND EXERCISES

ON MELANCHOLY

1. This ode is a fragment; its first stanza was never satisfactorily completed, and like Coleridge's *Dejection*, it is a poem of self-revelation, as is also the Nightingale Ode. Does it seem to you that melancholy is a part of Keats's outlook on life?

2. In a letter to his brother, Keats wrote:

With a great poet the sense of beauty overcomes every other consideration, or rather obliterates all consideration.

Examine these four odes in the light of this statement.

ON THE BEACH AT NIGHT

1. Here is a poem composed in a different form from those that have gone before it. Consider the form.

2. Could we call this poem an *Ode on Immortality*, and could it be re-written in stanzaic form without loss of beauty?

ODE ON THE DEATH OF THE DUKE OF WELLINGTON

1. Examine the use of (*a*) repetition of the idea; (*b*) compound words in this ode.

2. The poet seems to try to suggest a funeral procession by the movement of his verse. Do you think he succeeds in doing this?

3. Consider the poet's use and treatment of historical fact in this poem, and compare it with Gray's use of history in *The Bard*.

WESTMINSTER ABBEY

1. Here again we have the utilisation of legend and history as a background. Compare with Tennyson's use in the preceding ode.

QUESTIONS AND EXERCISES

2. Do you find anything of the influence of Milton and Wordsworth in this ode?

3. "Gravity and a high and delicate seriousness are among the characteristics of Arnold's verse." Would you agree with this statement?

ODE TO THE NORTH-EAST WIND

1. Kingsley was the "apostle of muscular Christianity." Does the ode suggest this?

2. How different in treatment from Shelley's *Ode to the West Wind*!

3. Does the movement of the verse at all suggest the strength and harshness of the wild north-easter?

TO VICTOR HUGO

1. What is Swinburne's estimate of Victor Hugo so far as it finds expression in this ode?

2. Consider the form of the stanza. Can you name any poem which may have suggested it to the poet?

3. It would be well to read the choric songs written by Swinburne for his Greek tragedies, *Atalanta in Calydon* and *Erechtheus*. See especially the song of the Spring in *Atalanta*, and in *Erechtheus*, the song of Storm and Battle commencing "Let us lift up the strength of our hearts in song," and Oreithyia, "Out of the north wind grief came forth," etc.

ODE BY O'SHAUGHNESSY

1. Of whom is the poet writing? Do the poems in this book bear out his claim?

2. The rhythm employed is worthy of analysis.

QUESTIONS AND EXERCISES

WINTER

1. "Patmore had a real love of Nature, and a deep understanding of her ways." Can you gather this from this ode?

2. This poem is from a volume of odes, *The Unknown Eros*, which form an epic of modern love. Many of these odes are well worth study, *e.g.*, *To the Unknown Eros, The Toys, Departure, If I were Dead, The Child's Purchase*, and others.

APPENDIX

TRANSLATIONS OF PINDARIC AND HORATIAN ODES

OLYMP. I

TO HIERO, KING OF SYRACUSE, VICTOR IN THE HORSE-RACE

Translated by the Rev. F. D. Morice, M.A.

I

Strophe

Peerless is water. Gold, like flames that gleam
  In darkest night, doth proudest wealth outshine.
But oh! if contests be the theme
  Thou choosest, heart of mine!
    As soon expect some star more fair
    Shall yon bright sun outblaze in barren air,
As hope of sports to tell, Whose glories may excel
    Olympia, whence harmonious voices spring,
    That fire poetic souls to sing
The son of Cronus, when they come
To Hiero's proud and happy home.

Antistrophe

With rod of righteousness the fields he sways
  Of pastoral Sicily, and culls the prime
Of virtue, while around him blaze
  The brightest flowers of rime,
    Such festal lays as oft we wake
    Around his board. The Dorian lyre come take,
If haply Pisa's meed, That graced that victor steed,

Bright dreams of rapture o'er your spirit shed,
  As by Alphæus' banks he sped.
No need of spur—on, on he flies.
And bears his master toward the prize.

Epode

The lord of Syracuse, whose coursers' fame
Shines in the land where Lydian Pelops came,
  New home to found—Pelops, of ocean's king,
Poseidon, loved—whom Clotho drew From out the laver's
      cleansing dew
  With ivory shoulder glistening.
Marvels are many; yet still stranger tale,
With falsehood tricked, may oft o'er truth prevail.

II

Strophe

Favour (to whom all earthly joys are due),
  Brings credence oft, and well such art she plies
As makes the truthless tale seem true.
  But wiser faith relies
    On evidence of coming days.
    Yet errs the mortal least that speaks in praise
Of Gods—and newly thus, O son of Tantalus,
    I'll frame thy tale. What time on Sipylus' height
    Thy sire Heaven's favour did requite,
And called the Gods about his board;
Seized wert thou of the Trident's lord.

Antistrophe

Inspired with love, he bore thee far away,
  On shining steeds, to Zeus' exalted home:
Where, even so, in later day
  Did Ganymedes come
    To Zeus. And when no search might track
    Thy flight, nor bring thee to thy mother back;
Some jealous neighbour's tongue, A dark surmise outflung,

APPENDIX

And told how, at the cauldron's boiling point,
  With steel they cleft thee joint from joint,
Then round the board in portions spread
The seething flesh, and on thee fed.

Epode

I cannot tax blest Powers with greed so gross,—
I dare not. Oft is slander's gain but loss.
  And sure, if e'er Olympian watchers loved
A mortal, Tantalus was blest; Yet ill might he such bliss
      digest.
    So pride's excess his ruin proved.
  A massy stone did Zeus above him poise,
  To threaten aye his head, and banish joys.

III

Strophe

And thus he dwells, doomed with the toiling Three
    To hopeless pain; for, from immortals riven,
Ambrosia and nectar he
    To mortal guests had given,
        Whence deathless life himself had won.
        But whoso hopes his daring crimes may shun
    The sight of Heaven, is vain; And so the Gods again
        Sent back his son to join Man's fleeting race.
        And when the dark down fringed his face,
In earliest manhood's blossom-tide,
He duly sought a noble bride,

Antistrophe

Hippodamia, her Pisan father's boast.
    So to the Lord of ocean's roar he prayed
At midnight on the lone sea-coast.
    At once, his friend to aid,
        He saw the Trident-armed appear:
            And, "If," he cried, "our love hath made me dear,

"Poseidon, to thy heart; Oh, stay Oenomaus' dart.
 To Elis bear me in thy car apace,
 And make me victor in the race.
For thirteen suitors he hath slain,
His daughter's wedding to restrain.

Epode

"Yet direst perils bravest hearts befit.
Die must we all—then why in darkness sit,
 Chewing the cud of eld, unknown to fame,
Stranger to all that graces life? No; set am I to dare the strife;
 Fulfil thou then my cherished aim."
He spake, nor vainly prayed: Poseidon gave
His golden car, and winged coursers brave.

IV

Strophe

Oenomaus fell—and fell the maiden too,
 The victor's prize! Six royal sons she bare
To virtue dear; and now, with due
 Of sacrifices fair,
  He rests beside Alpheüs' wave,
  Hard by yon shrine, whose votaries throng his grave!
 And through Olympia's ring, the hero's glories fling
  Their beams afar; where rivals swift of feet,
  And deeds of hardiest prowess meet,
 And he, that conquers in the strife,
Wins sweetest peace for all his life,

Antistrophe

Far as may triumph bless; for nought so high
 As bliss renewed through every changing day.
But now the victor-chief must I
 Crown with Æolian lay,—

APPENDIX

  Chivalrous strain. And well I wot, that ne'er
   Shall living man, renowned for wisdom fair—
As he—and prowess bold, In song's bright coil be told.
   Thy patron deity, my Hiero, still
    Labours to grant thee all thy will:
  And, save he quit his post ere long,
  I trust with yet a sweeter song

EPODE

Thy rapid car to greet, and trace aright
Song's helpful path to Cronium's sunny height.
 Mine are the boldest shafts the Muses lend.
In divers fashions men are great, But highest soars the
    kingly state,
  No further man may gaze.
Tread thou such heights! And be it mine to dwell
Mid victors, and in song all Greeks excel!

THE FIFTH ODE OF HORACE. BOOK I

Translated by John Milton

 Rendered almost word for word, without rhyme, according to the Latin measure, as near as the language will permit.

What slender youth bedew'd with liquid odours
Courts thee on roses in some pleasant cave,
  Pyrrha for whom bind'st thou
  In wreaths thy golden hair,
Plain in thy neatness; O how oft shall he
On faith and changed Gods complain: and seas
  Rough with black winds and storms
  Unwonted shall admire:
Who now enjoys thee credulous, all gold,
Who always vacant, always amiable
  Hopes thee; of flattering gales
  Unmindful. Hapless they

To whom thou untried seem'st fair. Me in my vow'd
Picture the sacred wall declares t' have hung
    My dank and dropping weeds
      To the stern God of Sea.

THE NINTH ODE OF HORACE. BOOK I

Translated by John Conington

See how it stands, one pile of snow,
   Soracte! 'neath the pressure yield
Its groaning woods; the torrents' flow
   With sharp clear ice is all congeal'd.
Heap high the logs, and melt the cold,
   Good Thaliarch; draw the wine we ask,
That mellower vintage, four-year-old,
   From out the cellar'd Sabine cask.
The future trust with Jove; when He
   Has still'd the warring tempests' roar
On the vex'd deep, the cypress-tree
   And aged ash are rock'd no more.
O, ask not what the morn will bring,
   But count as gain each day that chance
May give you; sport in life's young spring,
   Nor scorn sweet love, nor merry dance,
While years are green, while sullen eld
   Is distant. Now the walk, the game,
The whisper'd talk at sunset held,
   Each in its hour, prefer their claim.
Sweet too the laugh, whose feign'd alarm
   The hiding-place of beauty tells,
The token, ravish'd from the arm
   Or finger, that but ill rebels.

THE END